BOBBY

FAMILY FRIENDLY HOME BIBLE STUDY

VOLUME ONE
THE BOOKS OF THE LAW

21ST CENTURY
PRESS
PUBLISHING WITH PURPOSE
WWW.21STCENTURYPRESS.COM

FAMILY FRIENDLY HOME BIBLE STUDY

VOLUME ONE

THE BOOKS OF THE LAW

ISBN 0-9749811-5-X

Cover: Lee Fredrickson
Book Design: Terry White
Visit our website at: www.21stcenturypress.com

21ST CENTURY
PRESS
PUBLISHING WITH PURPOSE
WWW.21STCENTURYPRESS.COM

ACKNOWLEDGEMENTS

To Dianne, Christa, Nathan, and Charity. These are the greatest people in my life. Through the years, they have been a constant joy and a source of encouragement to my life and the lives of others that they have touched. To Verne Brummel, whose scholarship motivated within me a desire to touch others with the Word of God in a "Simple Way." Then, to Ken, Diane, and Robbie Lazar, who without their prayers and support, this book would only be a dream. Thanks guys! Only eternity will tell what God was able to do with this offering of love. Its been a great journey.

THE PENTATEUCH

(THE FIRST FIVE BOOKS OF THE BIBLE)

G	E	L	N	D
E	X	E	U	E
N	O	V	M	U
E	D	I	B	T
S	U	T	E	E
I	S	I	R	R
S		C	S	O
		U		N
		S		O
				M
				Y

THIS BOOK BELONGS TO:_____

TABLE OF CONTENTS

FOREWORD

As you begin to study the first five books of the Bible, you cannot help but wonder: "Why study these books? Isn't it just ancient history? What could I possibly learn from events that happened so long ago? This is the space age where everything is modernized and updated, so what can I get out of this study?"

In I Corinthians 10:6 & 11 we read, "Now these things occurred as examples..." What things occurred? The events that we are about to study together occurred so that we can learn from our forefathers some important truths about our God that would enable us to live a more pleasing, holy, and righteous life before Him.

Let us not be "ignorant" like many others who refuse to learn from these examples and therefore cause much heartache and pain to the One who loves us. But as we study these five books together, let us have open hearts as God speaks to us through His story of His chosen people.

My God bless you richly as you study His Word.

—Dr. Bobby W. Winkler, Jr.

SUMMARY OF THE BIBLE

Before we begin this journey of studying the Bible, it is very important that we see how the Bible came to us. The Bible was written by about forty men during a period of 1500 years, from the period of 1500 B.C. to A.D.100. The Bible was written not in the words of man's wisdom but in the words taught by the Holy Spirit. This is recorded in I Corinthians 2:13 and 2 Peter 1:21.

The English Bible which we have is divided up into ten sections. The Old Testament is broken up into five consisting of thirty-nine books within itself. These books are arranged as follows;

The Books of the Law=The Pentateuch or Torah-consisting of five books called, Genesis, Exodus, Leviticus, Numbers, and Deuteronomy.

The History Books=The Conquest Books-consisting of twelve books called, Joshua, Judges, Ruth, I&II Samuel, I&II Kings, I&II Chronicles, Ezra, Nehemiah, and Esther.

The Poetical Books=The Wisdom Literature-consisting of five books called, Job, Psalms, Proverbs, Ecclesiastes, and Song of Solomon.

The Major Prophets=The Pre-Exilic Prophets-consisting of five books called Isaiah, Jeremiah, Lamentation, Ezekiel, and Daniel.

The Minor Prophets=The Post-Exilic Prophets-consisting of twelve books called: Hosea, Joel, Amos, Obadiah, Jonah, Micah, Nahum, Habakkuk, Zephaniah, Haggai, Zechariah, and Malachi.

The New Testament is broken up into five sections as well. They are arranged as follows:

The Four Gospels=   The Four Sides of the Good News of Jesus Christ-consisting of four books called: Matthew, Mark, Luke, and John.

The History book of the Church=The Acts of the Apostles and Paul. Consisting of the Book of Acts only.

The Pauline Epistles=The Letters to the church from Paul consisting of fourteen books called: Romans,   I&II   Corinthians, Galatians, Ephesians, Philippians, Colossians,   I&II   Thessalonians,

I&II Timothy, Titus, Philemon, Hebrews.

The General Epistles=The letters from the other Apostles consisting of seven books called: James, I&II Peter, I, II, & III John, and Jude.

The Book of Prophecy=the Apocalyptic book of the end of the world and the future of mankind. This book is called Revelation.

The Hebrew Bible

The Hebrew Bible in contrast is divided up into three sections. There are the first five books of Law. There is the section labeled the eight books of the Prophets which is split into the two categories entitled Former and Latter Prophets. The last section of the Hebrew Bible is called the Writings. It has three Poetical books, five Scrolls and three historical books of Israel.

The Central Theme of the Bible

The central theme of the Bible is Jesus Christ. "The whole Bible is built around the story of Christ and His promise of life everlasting to men. It was written only that we might believe and understand, know, love, and follow Him." The word "testament" means "a promise or agreement." The Old Testament is the covenant God made with man about his salvation coming. Christ came. The New Testament is the agreement that God made with man about his salvation in that Christ has come. In the Old Testament we find the covenant of blood. In the New Testament we find the covenant of grace.

The History of the Bible

As far as history, the Bible contains the history from Adam to Abraham concerning the human race. It contains the history of the faith race from Abraham to Christ. Then we have the history of the church and we thus see that the Bible is about "His Story!" The Bible teaches and deals with what we call the "Foundational Truths of the Bible." Areas are also called the "Fundamentals of the Faith." In other words, all true Christians believe the same on these ten areas. These areas are as follows; God, Jesus Christ, The Holy Spirit, Satan, Man, Sin, Demons, Salvation, The Church, and Future things.

As you study the Bible, there are several ways that you can do this. You can study the Bible by chapters. You can study it verse-by-verse, by paragraphs, by book, or topically.

Before you can accurately study the Bible, you must first seek the direction of the One who wrote it. It has been said,"When we pray, it is us talking to God and when we read and study the word, it is God talking to us."

We call this "Quiet Time." A Quiet time is a brief time

daily, alone with God. It is listening to Him through His Word and talking to Him in prayer. Quiet time gives you an opportunity to realize God's presence, to praise him, to dedicate yourself to His service that day. It is also a time to ask Him to meet your own needs and the needs of others. There is a simple acrostic that helps when we are going to pray. It is as follows;

A=Adore Him--Let God know how special He is to you.
C=Confession of Sin, even if you can't remember it!
T=Thanksgiving-Just thanking Him for all things good
        or bad.
S=Supplication-Sharing our dreams, desires and love for
        others With God.

After praying, then get into the Word and see what insights and direction God gives. Meditation. Be still and know that He is God. Listen quietly to the "still small voice of God." Then do the "So What" application. How can I obey what God has given me in my Quiet time today? After all this, pray a prayer of obedience and dedication of what God is going to do now. Then share with someone else what God has taught you this day (I John 1:3).

INTRODUCTION TO THE PENTATEUCH

The word *Pentateuch* is actually a Greek word which means the "Five Scrolls." It is also called the "Torah" or "Books of God's Law." The Pentateuch has also been called the "Book of Moses." The human author is Moses and the real author is God the Holy Spirit. See Old Testament passages such as Ex. 17:14; 24:4-8; Num. 33:1,2; Deut. 31:9,22,24; I Kings 2:3; II Kings 14:6; Ezra 6:18; Neh. 13:1. The New Testament passages are; Mt. 19:8; Mk. 1:44; 10:4-5; Lk. 5:14; 16:31; 20:7; Acts 3:22; 13:39; 15:5; 26:22; Rom. 10:5, 19; I Cor. 9:9; II Cor. 3:15; Rev. 15:3.

The theme of the Pentateuch is three-fold. Historically, it records the origins of the human race and the origins and early fortunes of the human race. Legislatively, it records the laws that God gave to the Hebrew nation. And spiritually, it records God's work in history and His power over history.

An overall view will show that Genesis is about firsts. Genesis records the beginning of everything. In Exodus we have freedom from sin and this world in the ending of Jewish slavery to the mighty Egyptian empire. In Leviticus we have the rules for living and God's call for the Jewish people to fully consecrate or give themselves to God's way of living. Numbers recounts the history of Israel and the lessons that they had supposedly learned. Then, in Deuteronomy we see the law re-stated so that Israel mind have victory in a new land.

Where does Christ fit in these Old Testament books? Well, in Genesis we see Jesus portrayed as the Creator God. In Exodus we see Jesus portrayed as the Redeeming Savior. In Leviticus we see Jesus portrayed as the substitute for sin. In Numbers we see Jesus as the Commissioning Leader. Then finally in Deuteronomy we see Jesus as the Abiding Counselor.

INTRODUCTION TO GENESIS

The Author of course is Moses. The book of Genesis was written from Mt. Sinai. It was written between 1450 and 1410 B.C. It is the first book in the Bible and it displays God's role as The Creator of all things. God's command is stated in the first part of Genesis 1:1, "IN THE BEGINNING." The Key verse then would be Genesis 1:1. "In the beginning, God created the heaven and the earth." The Key message would be, "The wonder of a forgiving God and the tragedy of trusting human person." The key word of Genesis is "Beginnings." In Genesis 1:1-25 we have recorded the beginning of Heaven and Earth. In Genesis 1:26-2:25 we see the beginning of man and animals. In Genesis 3:1-7, we see the beginning of sin and shame. In Genesis 3:8-24 we see God's forgiveness and redemption. In Genesis 4:1-9:29, the progression of mankind and civilization as we know it. In Genesis 10:1-32, we the preservation of the races. In Genesis 11:1-9 we see the division of the nations. In Genesis 12-50, we have the family history of Abraham starting and nation and Joseph preserving a nation by Faith.

An Outline of the Book of Genesis is as follows:

I. The Focus On Events 1-11
   A. Creation 1, 2
   B. The Fall 3-5
   C. The Flood 6-9
   D. The Tower of Babel 10-11

II. The People Displayed 12-50
   A. Abraham-Friend of God 12-24
   B. Isaac-The Beloved Son 25-27
   C. Jacob-Changed to Israel 28-36
   D. Joseph-From Gloom to Glory 37-50

Genesis is the seed plot of the whole Bible. It is the foundation on which the divine revelation rests and on which it is built up. It is the key book of the Bible. If you do not accept this book as God-inspired, you will not be able to accept the rest of the bible as God-inspired.

Part I

FOCUS ON EVENTS

(GENESIS 1-11)

LESSON 1

CREATION

Chapters 1 and 2

Genesis 1:1 tells us where God came from. This verse tells us that God has always been and will always be. It does not argue the existence of God, but just takes for granted that the reader believes and understands that God exists. Hebrews 11:3 teaches us that all we have to do is look around at the physical things that God has made, and these things alone let the observer know that the things that appear did not just happen. Creation is a planned and orderly action. God does things on purpose. The phrase, "In the beginning God created..." teaches us that God himself was before creation. God is a personal being in that He takes great concern in what He creates. This is the foundational truth of all theology.

Genesis 1:3-2:24 focuses on God and His work, not on man and self. The chart below shows the reader that God created man to have dominion and right relationships with the other created things, whether it be man or his environment. The principle of relationships is this: "We can't be right with others if we are not right with God. In Genesis 1:3-5, we see the creation of light and darkness. In Genesis 1:6-8, we have the divisions of the water. In Genesis 1:9-13, we see the creation of the land and seas.

Genesis 1:14-19 records for us the sun, moon and the stars. In Genesis 1:20-23, we see animals created. Then in Genesis 1:24-31, the crown of God's creativity is displayed. It is the creation of Man. In Genesis 2:2-3, God rests. Each creation according to God was "good." But the creation nearest to God's heart was the creation of man. In Genesis 1:26-28, we see that the pronoun "us" refers to more than one person, but in a singular form. Isaiah 40:14 teaches us that no one consulted with God when it came to creation. The word used in Genesis 1:26 is also used in Isaiah 40:14.

There is another verb used in Hebrews 11. It tells is that by "faith" the worlds were made by God. So not only do we have the created world as physical evidence, we have the inner "still small voice" of the Holy Spirit that confirms to us that there is a God, and that this God personally cares about us.

One at this point might ask; "What is faith?" An acrostic can help us here. Faith is:
1) Following Jesus' Word unreservedly.
2) Asking, with trust that He knows best.
3) Instantly obeying without delay.
4) Trusting it is done.
5) Hoping and hanging in there no matter how you feel.

Hebrews 11:1 teaches us that "faith is the substance of things hoped for, the evidence of things not seen." This verse tells us three things that are important. It says that faith has substance. It is real, but not in the world that we know it to be, but it is just as real. Faith is hoped for. That is, that which we do not see becomes visible when we activate our steps by obedience. It is the believer's obedience to the unseen principles of God that make the unseen, seen. This last statement is thus summed up with these words, "the evidence of things not seen." So then faith is simply taking God at His word.

According to Hebrews 11:3, faith helps us to believe what we cannot see. Hebrews 11:6 then tells us that without faith it is impossible to please God. So why is faith so important? Well, you cannot be saved without faith (John 3:16). You cannot live a victorious life without faith (I John 2:17). You cannot please God without faith (Hebrews 11:6). You cannot ask right without faith (James 1:6). You cannot have peace without faith (Romans 5:1). You cannot have joy without faith (I Peter 1:8). You are justified by faith and not by works (Galatians 2:16). You are made righteous by faith (Romans 10:1-4). Christ dwells in your heart by faith (Ephesians 3:17). The Holy Spirit is received by faith (Galatians 3:2). In Romans 14:23, the Bible teaches that "whatsoever is not of faith is sin." Faith says, "I will trust and obey God even though I cannot see Him, for I know His Word is true." It also says, "When I cannot see God's hand, I can trust His heart, for God makes no mistakes." Faith is important, for it tells God that we trust Him!

In Genesis 1:26-31 and 2:15-17, we see how man was

formed. According to Genesis 1:26, man was formed in God's image. Man was at this time given authority over all of God's creation. The phrase "created in God's own image" means that man possesses those unique qualities of God that separate man from the rest of God's creation; the one main difference being the "soul." In verse 28 of Genesis one, man was commanded to be fruitful, multiply, replenish, and have dominion over all the earth. God would take care of man by giving him every tree in the Garden of Eden except one. This forbidden tree was known as "The Tree of the Knowledge of Good and Evil." We would do well to remember that God has boundaries not to keep us in, but to keep things out. In Genesis 2:18-23, we see the creation of woman. She was created by God to be Adam's companion and helper. Eve (mother of all living), was taken from the rib of Adam. It has been said that woman was taken out from under the arm of man so that man could protect, provide, and lead woman. She was not taken from man's foot to be walked over, kicked, and left behind. Eve was called woman for she came from man's heart. At this point, the first institution was made.

This institution would be called "marriage." See and read Genesis 2:23-24.

Word Study:

    A. Hovering (1:2): To protect and inspect.

    B. Expanse (1:6): Vast and wide

    C. Teeming (1:21): To be abundant in life.

    D. Subdue (1:28): To have control of.

    E. Vast (2:1): A wide open large area.

    F. Array (2:1): To be decorated with full color.

Project: List and Illustrate the Days of Creation.

Just a Note: The "Image of God" means the ability to think, act intelligently, and worship God. Man has a soul that lives for eternity in Heaven or Hell, based on his choice about the finished work of Christ. Man is existent; he never ceases to be. The Trinity, even though not specifically mentioned, is taught in Genesis 1:26-28. The word "Trinity" means "Three distinct persons, but only one God." God the Father is clearly seen as the Creator. God the Son is clearly seen as the Executor of Life. God the Holy Spirit is clearly seen as the Inspector and Intelligence of man. In the Old Testament, God is called Jehovah. In the New Testament, God is called Jesus. In the church age, God is called the Holy Spirit. However, all three are still one God even today.

Devotional Reading: Genesis 1 and 2

Memory Verse: Genesis 1:1, 2, 27

THE FATAL FALL

Chapters 3-5

In Genesis chapter 3:1,4,5,14, we see Satan in the form of a serpent. The serpent is described as being "more subtle than any beast of the field." The word "subtle" means thin, sleek, cunning, and deceitful. We know that this describes Satan. He asked the woman a question. Did God say not to eat of every tree of the garden? No! He said not to eat of the Tree of the Knowledge of Good and Evil. Satan then  tells Eve that she shall not die. This was a lie, for man would surely die one day, both physically and spiritually, the moment man disobeyed God. The Bible talks about three types of death: There is a **physical death**. Physical death is when all bodily functions stop working. There is a **spiritual death**. This type of death is what all mankind experiences today without Jesus Christ. Then there is a **second death**. This is when all the lost will be condemned to the lake of fire for eternity! God curses man to work by the" sweat of his brow." Woman is promised pain in child birth and submission to the man as leader. The serpent is cursed above all cattle and above every beast of the field. The serpent went from a desirous creature to a hideous beast. The serpent would crawl on his belly, and the dust and dirt would be his food. Satan was earlier cast out of Heaven after trying to lead one-third of the angels against God in Heaven. His place of habitat would be the realm of Earth. In Isaiah 14:12-15, the reader can well see why Satan was cast out of Heaven. It is a bad thing when we get ahead of God. Pride has ruined many great people. Satan said, "I will ascend into Heaven; I will exalt my throne above the stars of God; I will sit also upon the mount of the congregation; I will ascend above the heights of the clouds; I will be like the Most High!"

The Bible teaches several things about Satan. He was created as one of the Cherub Angels (Ezekiel 28:12-15). Satan fell from his heavenly estate through his rebellious attitude (Isaiah 14:12-15). God promises Satan ultimate defeat through the "seed of the woman" (Genesis 3:15). Jesus called Satan the "prince of this world" (John 14:30). In his own time, God's full wrath will come upon Satan (Revelation 20:10).

In Genesis 3:2,3,6,7,13,16,20, Eve saw that the tree was good for food. This was a temptation of the flesh. The tree was pleasant to the eyes. This was a temptation of the eyes. The tree was desired to make one wise. This last part was a temptation of the life. If we compare Genesis 3:6-7 with I John 2:16, one can see the three areas of attack that Satan uses against people. After Eve ate the fruit, she gave it to Adam to eat. Notice Eve's pattern of sin. **She saw**: Eve should have turned away—a great deal of sin comes in through the eyes! **She took**: This was her own act or deed—Satan may tempt, but he does not force the issue.

She did eat: Perhaps she did not intend to eat it when she looked, but this was the result. **She did offer it to Adam**: Eve persuaded Adam with the same arguments that the serpent used with her. No sooner  a sinner than a tempter. **He did eat**: Adam chose to disobey God (Romans 5:19). Eve then plays the "blame game." Eve, when confronted by God as to why she disobeyed, blamed the serpent. As He said He would do earlier in the text, God then placed a curse of sorrow and pain in childbirth, and submission to the man as the leader of the home. Woman was then called "Eve"—the mother of all living. In chapter 3:9-12, we find man hiding. This is an unnatural result of guilt. We need to remember that guilt is Satan's way of getting us away from God. Conviction is God's way of bringing us to Himself for help. Why was Adam hiding? He knew that he had done wrong. Instead of taking responsibility, Adam blames Eve. For this, God the Father sentenced man to hard labor and difficulties the rest of his days. What were the results from all this disobedience? God would make the clothes by killing an innocent animal. Our sin does hurt those around us! God had to send both man and woman out of the garden and

put angels and a flaming sword out by its gate.

In Genesis 4:1-16, we have the first murder. Sadly enough, it was family connected. It involved a man who killed his own flesh and blood! In verse two of Genesis 4, we see Abel, the younger brother, who was a shepherd or keeper of sheep. His older brother Cain was a farmer. Both were asked to give God a sacrifice. By this time, God had set the standard of what type of sacrifice was needed to cover their sin. It was the death of an animal. Abel offered to God an animal sacrifice. Cain offered to God a plant sacrifice. In verses 5-7, we see God's response. Abel's sacrifice was accepted. Cain's sacrifice was not accepted. Why was Abel's sacrifice accepted over Cain's? According to Hebrews 9:22 and 11:4, blood was the payment for sin.

A good note to remember: when God tells us what to do, we have but one way to do it. It is to do exactly what God says and how God says to do it. To disobey is to sacrifice more than we want to sacrifice (I Samuel 15:22). In chapter 4:8-15, Cain is so mad at God that he becomes jealous of his brother Abel and ends up murdering his brother. When a man or woman is out of fellowship with God, they are dangerous to themselves and others. Cain did not want to accept his responsibility. If there is anything we need today in this present world, it is for people to take responsibility for their actions.

Word Study:

A. Crafty: (3:1)-Cunning and sneaky

B. Enmity: (3:15)-Division and at war

C. Banished: (3:23)-Sent out away from

D. Cherubim: (3:24)-Guardian Angel of God's holiness

E. Crouching: (4:7)-Lying in wait for

F. Vengeance: (4:15)-To get back or repay for something

G. Forged: (4:22)-Carved into with pressure

Basic Truths:

A. "Spiritual Death"-the state of relationship with God in which a person is separated from God through disobedience, rebellion, trespass, and sin (Eph. 2:1).

B. Every sin has its consequences!

Devotional Reading: Genesis 3,4:1-16

Memory Verse: Genesis 3:15, John 3:16-17

THE FLOOD THAT CHANGED THE WORLD

(Genesis 6-9)

In these next three chapters, we see the judgment of God on mankind. This happens in chapters 6 and 7. Verses 1-4 record what mankind was like in order for God to have to execute judgment. The sons of God saw the daughters of men and were lead away by the beauty of the daughters of men. Another thing that happened was that the sons of God intermarried with the daughters of men. God put up with this ungodliness for 120 years. In verse 5-13, we see that the wickedness of man covered the earth. In verse 7, God decides to destroy man from the earth. Verse 8 tells us that there was only one man who was righteous in the sight of God, and that man was Noah. Noah was a just, fair, and honorable man. Noah was perfect, meaning that Noah was mature in his living before God. Noah walked with God. We see all this in verse 9. In Genesis 6:14-22, God provides a way of salvation for Noah. God asks Noah to make an "Ark." Ark is Hebrew for box or coffin. This ark would be a symbol of safety in the God of Israel. It also symbolizes the death of a believer to this world. God instructed Noah to build the Ark and pitch it within and without. The ark would be 450 feet long, 45 feet high, and 475 feet long . In chapter 7:1-24,

God begins His work to "clean up" the sin of man. He allowed the rain to fall for 40 days and 40 nights. God would miraculously bring the animals to the ark.

God would bring seven clean animals into the ark for food and sacrifices. God would also bring two of the

unclean animals to preserve the species. After the water had risen to its highest level, all mankind would be destroyed. Noah and his family stayed in the ark for 375 days, or one year and ten days. In chapter 8:21, God makes a promise to Noah that the world would never again be destroyed by water. God gave the rainbow as a symbol of his promise to man. Every time man sees a rainbow, it reminds him of God's promise. The next time God's judgment comes, it will be by fire, according to II Peter 3:5-12.

Word Study:
   A. Mortal (6:3)-Humans
   B. Inclination (6:5)-The urge to do something.
   C. Favor (6:8)-In good standing.
   D. Righteous (6:18)-Right before God.
   E. Covenant (7:2)-A promise or agreement.
   F. Clean Animals (7:2)-Jewish law that separated certain animals for food and sacrifices.
   G. Unclean Animals (7:2)-Jewish law that prohibits this type of animals.
   H. Recede (8:5)-To go down or back.

Project: Draw a picture of the Ark (include: door, window, dimensions, water, and the rainbow, etc...)

Devotional Reading: Genesis 6:1-9:17

Memory Verse: Hebrews 11:6-7

Basic Truths: There are seven covenants found in the Bible: The Adamic Covenant (Genesis 2:16-17); The Noahic Covenant (Genesis 9:8-13); The Abrahamic Covenant (Genesis 12:1-3); The Mosaic Covenant (Exodus 19:5).

There is the Restoration Covenant (Deuteronomy 30:3-10); The Davidic Covenant (II Samuel 7:16); The Messianic Covenant (Hebrews 8:8). Another basic truth is that God hates sin. He must punish sin because He is just and holy.

Just a Note: Compare Genesis 9:6 and Romans 13:4. How should one interpret these verses? Look up these verses.

1. Leviticus 24:16_____
2. Numbers 15:30-31_____
3. Exodus 22:18_____
4. Leviticus 20:10_____
5. Exodus 21:16_____
6. Leviticus 20:2_____

B. How was capital punishment carried out?
1. Numbers 25:4; Deuteronomy 21:22_____
2. Leviticus 20:27_____
3. Matthew 14:10; Acts 12:2_____
4. Genesis 38:24_____

Question: Is capital punishment for today?

LESSON 4

TRYING TO REACH GOD
THE WRONG WAY

(Genesis 11:1-9)

Unity can be a beautiful and productive thing if handled and nurtured in the cradle of humility. Let man's pride get into the way and you have nothing short of human anarchy. The thing that was unique about this time of history is that the whole world spoke one language. As one thinks about the culture, what language did these ancients speak? Some believe it was Sumerian. We come to  this conclusion because one of the oldest languages besides Chinese is ancient Sumerian. From this culture came the culture of the Chaldeans. Abraham was from the city of Ur. His language was Chaldean. Another speculation is that of Hebrew. Some think that Hebrew came from a mixture of Sumerian, Arabic, and Phoenician. One thing is for sure, one may never really know the language, but we do know that at the time of the building of the Tower of Babel, the whole world was connected with one language. We know from verse 4 that the people of Babel were building a tower to reach heaven. Man has an inner desire to be with, or like God. Only God can fill the emptiness that is in man. However, there was only one way given to reach God and it was by faith and not the works of man's hands. We also see that the people of Babel were interested in making themselves a name. In verse 6, God had to stop the people of Babel from building, because they were not interested in a personal fellowship with God by faith. Man has always wanted to touch God, but on man's level. God cannot be approached by sinful man in his sin, but through the perfection of God's grace and mercy. There was only one way to God, and that is through faith in the shed blood of Jesus Christ (Hebrews 9:22, Ephesians 2:8-9). We find that God comes down and sees the evil and selfish intentions of man and decides to confuse their language, thus giving us the name "Babel."

Babel means "confusion, and to ramble or babble on without understanding."

Basic Truths:
    A. Be very careful of your motives for doing things.
    B. Sin causes confusion between God and man.

Devotional Reading: Genesis 11:1-9
Memory Verse: Genesis 11:6

Part II

FOCUS ON PEOPLE

GENESIS 12-50

LESSON 5

SURRENDERING TO THE VOICE OF GOD

Chapters 12-17

Abram's Call (11:27-12:20)

Abraham was born in the city of Ur, which was a Sumerian city. From what we know, Ur was a poly-theistic society. Worship was done from on top of "Ziggurat" type temples where worship of the Zodiac, or worship of the planets was popular. The Bible does not go into detail as to Abraham's origin. However, we do have the account where Abraham heard the voice of God and obeyed Him. When God told Abraham to follow God, he did so by faith. We have record of Abram's father, Nahor, and where he died. According to Genesis 11:31, Nahor died in Haran. After Nahor's death, Abram left and traveled south to a place called Canaan. In Genesis 12:10, we see that there arose a famine in the land of Canaan. This famine caused Abram to go into the land of Egypt. Leaving family was not easy because it meant that one was leaving the loving protection and security that they had enjoyed. By faith, Abram obeyed God. Sometimes it is not easy to step out by faith and leave the security of those you love. Faith and obedience lead to the blessings and spiritual growth that awaits those who want to know God. It is far better to leave with God to an unknown

41

place that is His perfect will, than it is to stay around and be a problem to self and others because of unbelief and disobedience.

Abram's Separation From Nephew Lot (Genesis 13)

Abram took his nephew, Lot, with him when he was

supposed to leave family. Sometimes, family can be a problem, if not surrendered to the will and authority of God and his leader. Why is this so? It takes a very strong and humble family to be in subjection to a family member who is a leader. Sometimes, if not careful, family members can demand special treatment in some situations. This is the case with Lot. His interest lay not in the things of simplicity or godliness. Lot's love was on what he could get for himself. Spiritual aspects meant nothing to Lot. We see this in verse 6. God had blessed Abram and Lot to the point that Lot's men and Abram's men were fighting over land. Lot was approached by Abram to work out the land and space problems. Abram gave Lot the first choice as to where he wanted to live. Lot chose the Jordan River valley.

Lot looked and saw the "well-watered" plains of

Jordan. The Bible says that Lot "pitched" his tent towards the city of Sodom and Gomorrah. Verse 13 tells us that Sodom and Gomorrah were wicked cities and very sinful. We know that the city was the downfall of Lot, for his thinking was greatly influenced by the men of the city. Today, young people and adults as well, would do well to remember that we are are greatly influenced by the company we keep! This is a sad story of a man who thought more of his ambition and popularity than he did the spiritual growth and future of his own family. Lot displays the downward spiral of sin. He looked, he lingered, he lost his family and self-respect. More than this, Lot lost the opportunity to lead the most important group of people in his life. Lot lost his family!

Abram's Loyalty to Lot (Chapter 14)

In this passage of scripture, we see what it means to care about others more than yourself. Here Abram goes to war to free his nephew from four kings. Abram has the favor of God. He wins, but takes no reward from the king of Sodom and Gomorrah. One would think that Lot would get the idea that the Sodomites were not the kind of people to hang around with. Some people never learn until tragedy takes place. This would be the lot of Lot.

Abram's Covenant (Chapter 15)

This chapter discloses the challenge of a new found faith, and what can happen when we do not wait on the

Lord's timing. In verse three, Abram reminds God that Abram has no child to pass on the family lineage. God's response was that Abram would indeed have an heir,and that this heir would have a family that was as the number of the stars in the heavens. Abram and Sarai doubted. Doubt today, still hope for the future!

Abram's Inconsideration (Chapter 16)

Sarai takes her handmaid Hagar, who was an Egyptian, and gives her to Abram so that a child can be born to both Abram and Sarai. Anytime that we get ahead of God, our plans will fail miserably. In verse 11, Hagar has a son,and they name him Ishmael. Ishmael grew up to become a hunter or outdoorsman. His name would also represent hatred, bitterness, and trouble in the future for the true son of Abram. The reason it was so important for a woman to have children, especially male children, is that this was how the blessing was handed down from one generation to the next. Not to have a man child as first born was embarrassing, but not to have children at all was looked down on by the society of that day. It was traditionally alright to have a slave that could bear children for the owner. Was it morally right in the sight of God? No! Dr. Bob Jones used to say, "It's never right to do wrong in order to do right." Sarai and Abram were trying to control their future themselves instead of waiting on God. God is never too early, nor too late. He is always right on time!

Abram's New Life (Chapter 17)

According to verse 1, Abram is now about ninety-nine years old. Sarai is probably ninety at this time. God comes to Abram one day and fulfills His promise to Abram. To signify this new life, God changes Abram's name to Abraham which means " father of many nations." God also changes Sarai's name to Sarah, which means " mother of many nations." In verses 7-8, God makes an "everlasting covenant" with Abraham. God promised to take the seed of Abraham and multiply it. Out of this seed would come a mighty nation of people who would be  His people, and He would be their God. In verse 16, God reminds this couple that kings would come from their seed. Abraham's response was falling on his face and laughing. Abraham then suggested that Ishmael would be a good choice, since Ishmael was already born. Many times, our picks are not God's. God sees the heart of each individual no matter what the outside says. He hears Sarah laughing and asks Abraham why Sarah laughed. She tries to deny it, but God hears all things. God now pronounces that a son would be born in Sarah's old age.

The son's name would be called Isaac.

Word Study:
    A. Accumulated (12:5)-To gain things.
    B. Famine (12:10)- No food in the land.
    C. Subject (14:4)- To be under authority.
    D. Allied (14:5)- To be on the same side.
    E. Estate (15:2)- inheritance left.
    F. Hostility (16:12)- Ill feelings that lead to harmful actions.
    G. Circumcised (16:10)- Jewish ceremonial right that cleansed and separated male Jewish babies.
    H. Blameless (17:1)- Nothing found wrong with.

Devotional Reading: Genesis 12, 13, 15, 16, 17

Memory Verse: Hebrews 11:8-10

LESSON 6

WHAT PRAYING FOR OTHERS LOOKS LIKE

Chapter 18-24

Abraham's Prayer (Chapter 18)

In chapter 18 of Genesis, three men bring Abraham news that Sarah would indeed have a son. In verse 12, Sarah is in her tent. As Sarah hears the news about her having a son, she laughs. God hears this laughter and asks why Sarah laughed. In verse 14, God reminds both Abraham and Sarah that nothing is too hard for the Lord. A good question to ask here is this; Do you believe this statement in verse 14? What are some things that have happened to you that you thought would never happen? Jehovah reminds Sarah that she would have this son, and that his name would be called Isaac, which means " he laughs." The remaining verse of this chapter shows what " intercessory prayer" looks like. Sodom and Gomorrah were very wicked cities. In verse 20, God tells Abraham that He fully intends to destroy these two cities of sin. Abraham begins to ask God if He would destroy the city if there were any righteous people living there. God's answer is NO! Abraham was concerned about Lot and any righteous people that might be in those two cities. Abraham gets God to promise that He would spare the city if only there were ten righteous people. How sad that there were none to be found. This was also a sad commentary on the witness of Lot.

Abraham's Prayer is Answered (Chapter 19:1-29)

Angels are sent to rescue Lot. The angels stay with Lot at his house. The men of the city hear that Lot has two "men" staying at his house. The Bible tells us that these men of Sodom and Gomorrah wanted Lot to send these two angels out so that the men of the city could get to know them. This sounds like an innocent gesture of friendship. In this case, the word "know," means "to have physical relations with." This is where we get our word for "sodomy." These men wanted then to have a physical relationship with the two angels!

Notes To Remember

Sodom and Gomorrah never occur more than 13 times in the Bible. They were great and exceedingly wicked. Genesis 13:11-13 gives a vivid description of these two cities. Chapter 21 reveals four things concerning God and His character. God is true to His promises. God will do what He says He will do! God is a God that truly cares about people. He took care of Ishmael and his mother Hagar. God is a God who hears our cries. He heard the cries of Hagar and her baby in the wilderness. He heard the cries of His people in Egyptian captivity. God heard the cries of Abraham for his nephew Lot. God has a plan for our lives.

If one could walk through the streets of Sodom and Gomorrah, what would they see? Through the eyes of Lot, "Here is my chance to make a name for myself and get rich!" Through the eyes of the Sodomites, "Why didn't Lot tell us about our judgment?" Through the eyes of God, "I love you, but I have given you a chance to repent of your evil ways." Through the eyes of Lot's family, "Dad, you did-n't care about us!" It is true, sin will cost you more than you want to pay, and take you farther than you want to go.

Lot bows to an all-time low when, in verse 8, Lot offers his own daughters in place of the angels. The men of the city did not accept Lot's offer. When you have a father like Lot, you don't need to have enemies. This shows how dangerous a "backslidden" person can be. When the men pressed to try and break Lot's door down, the angels blinded the men of the city. In verse 15, Lot, his two daughters, and wife are basically dragged out of the city. Looking back, Lot's wife was turned into a pillar of salt. Men cannot expect their wives to obey them if they them-selves will not obey God. Our families can be a mirror of our obedience to God by the way they respond to us as leaders. Verse 16 tells us that Lot was spared to continue his family line. Fire and brimstone are rained down upon Sodom and Gomorrah in verse 24. In verse 26, Lot's wife is turned into a pillar of salt.

The Bible has a lot to say about "homosexuality." Leviticus 18:22,29 says that homosexuality is an

abomination to God. It is an insult to God and His creation of man. Leviticus 20:13 says that a person will die
for the act of homosexuality. Romans 1:26 says that when
man will not listen, then God will give them up to their
own vile affections to receive in their bodies the payment
of their sin. I Corinthians 6:9 tells us that people who
practice homosexuality are not saved! I Timothy 1:10
teaches us that those who live in this sin, err from the
truth. Homosexuality is not the ultimate sin, but it is the
ultimate distortion of God's creative genius. Paul affixes
six terms of evaluation to this sin: He calls it unseemli-
ness, lust, dishonor, vile affections, against nature, and
shameful. Anyone involved in this vile wickedness falls
under the scope of God's judgment.

Abraham's Lie (Chapter 20)

There is a king in Canaan, and Abraham has to lie to
him to save his life. While in the king's presence, the king
sees Sarah and appreciates her beauty. The king asks
Abraham if she is his wife. Fearing for his life, Abraham
lies and says that Sarah is his sister. This was not totally a
lie, as far as being family related. Sarah was Abraham's
cousin. There are two truths to be seen here. In
Abraham's day, marriages were pre-arranged with other
distant family members to preserve the culture of that
family. Another truth is that "half the truth is still a lie."
We see that Abraham also lied about Sarah being his wife
to the Egyptian Pharaoh in Genesis 12.

Abraham's Joy (Chapter 21:1-20)

In this chapter we see that Sarah was approximately 90 years old. As mentioned earlier, Sarah named her son Isaac. After this event, Sarah, in verse 10, did not want Hagar around. She demanded that Abraham put Hagar and Ishmael out. This sin of Abraham and Sarah shows us what happens when we do not wait on God. They now have to deal with the effects of their presumptuousness and how it hurts others around them. One would do well to remember that there is no such thing as a "private" sin. Our sin does affect others. In verse twenty, we see that Ishmael grows up to be a skilled outdoorsman and archer.

Abraham's Test (Chapter 22:1-19)

This chapter is perhaps one of the greatest in the Bible, for it shows us why Abraham was called the " friend of God." Here we see many lessons on what faith looks like when put to the test. Isaac was an obedient son. During this time, Isaac was probably a young man in his twenties. He was lively, strong and probably youthfully muscular. His dad at this time was no match for Isaac physically. However, this was not a test of will power between father and son. It could have been, but Abraham had set the example early in Isaac's life of obeying God. God told Abraham to go to Mount Moriah. This is where the Mosque of Omar is today, in the city of Jerusalem. Here, Abraham was told that he must sacrifice Isaac to God. With much blessing comes a test to see who really owns our lives, and if we are truly reliant on the One who gives them to us. Once they reach the summit of Mount Moriah, Isaac asks his dad, "where is the lamb for the burnt offering?" Abraham's response was one of prophetic utterance. Abraham said, "God Himself will provide a sacrifice." And God did provide, not only then at that moment, but when Christ came to Calvary to die for the sin of the whole world. God did indeed give us His Son as our substitute (John 3:16).

In verse 10, God allows Abraham to go as far as to draw the knife to kill Isaac. In this moment of personal anguish and pain, and probable disappointment with God, Abraham passes the supreme obedience factor. At this

WHAT PRAYING FOR OTHERS LOOKS LIKE 53

moment, Abraham puts his seemingly blinded faith in the promise that God said a great nation would come from Isaac. Abraham believed God! At this moment, God steps from the hallways of glory and stops Abraham. In the thicket is a ram, stuck and bound by the bush. God kept his promise. We can always count on God to do what He says He will do. That alone should keep us trusting. Sometimes faith is floundering unless it is tested. Faith is our spiritual muscle that must be worked if we are to become a stronger person. God reminds Abraham that He would indeed make a great nation from Isaac. This we see in the last part of verse 18.

There might be some that would argue with this event and try to make God seem unfair and harsh. What one must realize is that everything belongs to God, no matter what it is. Once we can settle the "who has ownership" in our lives, the more clearer our paths will become. This would not be murder, for you see, God would never go against His own Word. God is the Word!

We can rest assure that what God tells us to do, we can do, and it will be alright. God would never ask us to sin. There are some that cast doubt on this passage of scripture because they cannot see how Isaac would have just let Abraham sacrifice him without a struggle. This is very simple to figure out. Isaac was obedient because his father had set the example in his own life of obedience. Children do as we do, not as we say. They may do as we say when young, but they grow up to match our works with our words! Abraham was able to bridle the fear, loneliness, hurt, and the doubt, with faith in the already true Word of God. God had led Abraham this far, and Abraham knew that God would not leave him now.

Abraham's Family (Chapter 23)

In this chapter, we have the death and burial of Sarah. At this time, Sarah leaves us at the age of 127 years. Abraham purchases a tomb in Macpelah among the children of Heth.

Abraham's Provision for Isaac (Chapter 24:1-67)

In this chapter, we see the importance of marrying in the will of God. Parents in the mid-east of the world are very careful as to who their children marry. The reason for this is two-fold. The parents want to preserve family beliefs, and they want to preserve family ways, fortunes, and values. This is very important. This should be equally important to believers today. Although we do not marry into our own fleshly families as a practice, we as believers are plainly told to marry within our own faith family. This we see in II Corinthians 6:14-18. Here in this passage, it is made very plain that believers and unbelievers are not to be joined in marriage. Why? Because of the two reasons stated above. Abraham sends his servant to look for a wife among his own kindred. He tells the servant not to get a wife from the Canaanites. The Canaanites were a very ungodly and vicious people.

We also see the true quality that should be looked for in a mate. The servant goes to Nahor, who is Abraham's uncle, and devises a test to see who would be an appropriate mate for his master's son. The test was one of servanthood. The right young lady, when asked to give water to drink, would give water to both animals and man. One was required and the other gesture would be one of the heart. He had no longer finished his prayer when Rebekkah came out and offered to serve both the servant and his camels. In verse 26, the servant is shown to be worshipping God. This is a proper response to the blessings of God. In verses 34-49, the servant talks to Rebekkah's family and tells them what happens. They could not refuse to let her go, for they knew that this was the hand of God. Again, in verse 52, they worship God for what has happened and set back to Canaan. As the servant and Rebekkah drew near home, they could see a lonely figure in the distance, down on his knees praying. Isaac had been praying for his life's mate. All young people would do well to pray about their mate. It is an investment worth its weight in this lifetime. In verse 67, we see Isaac's response. The Bible says that Isaac lifted up his eyes and saw Rebekkah coming, and it says that he loved her.

Love at first sight is possible if the heart has already seen the person by faith. We see from the servant's prayer that prayer is totally relying on God to meet our needs, and letting God know that we understand this.

Word Study:

    A. Knead (18:6)-To grind up

    B. Curds (18:8)-Flakes of oats

    C. Grevious (18:20)-Disturbing

    D. Sulfur (19:24)-Fire burning substance left after a fire

    E. Catastrophe (19:29)-Total devastation

    F. Weaned (21:8)-Old enough to walk

    G. Oath (24:6)-Commitment made by mouth

Basic Truths: Please look up these scriptural principles based on the life of Lot:

1. I Corinthians 5:9-11; II Thessalonians 3:6, 14-15-
2. I Corinthians 15:33-
3. Psalm 1:1-
4. Proverbs 1:10-16-
5. Proverbs 13:20-
6. II Corinthians 6:14-18-

Devotional Reading: Genesis 18-24

Memory Verses: Hebrews 11:11-12

GOD'S ANSWER TO AN EMPTY WOMB

Chapter 25:20-27:46

Isaac's Sons (25:10-34)

Like any marriage, there are going to be challenges that couples will come up against that will either strengthen or weaken their relationship. In verse 21, we find that Rebekkah cannot have children. Isaac's response was one that every husband would do well to repeat. Instead of letting his emotions get out of control, Isaac prays for his bride in verse 21a. God hears Isaac's prayer and makes Rebekkah pregnant with child. In verse 23, God makes a prediction that there would arise two nations from the womb. This meant that Rebekkah would have twins. These twins would be at odds with each other. This, of course, would be discouraging words. There would be two different groups of people according to verse 23b. One would be stronger, but the elder would serve the younger. In verse 25, we see the appearances of these two boys. One would be born with a lot of hair and red-skinned. This child was named Esau. The next child born would be holding onto the first child's ankle. This child was fair-skinned. This child would be called Jacob, which means "supplanter" or "deceiving one." This name would later not only describe the character of Jacob, but it would be his demise. In verse 27, we see that Esau was a hunter, and that Jacob would be a "tent dweller."

We also see in this chapter what "favoritism" can do to our children, for we learn that Isaac loved Esau, and Rebekkah loved Jacob. According to verse 29, we find that Esau was greatly hungry from a long day of hunting. One could get the idea that he was near to starving to death or acted like it. Jacob, seeing this, knew that this was the time to steal something that was dear to the first born.

The blessing of the father to the first born meant many things in biblical times. The "blessing" meant financial rewards and the oversight of the family's money. It meant the right and responsibility as the head of the home and the direction of the family. Maybe Jacob thought that the "no care" attitude of Esau meant that the blessing of his family would be misused. Maybe Jacob felt that the blessing of his father Isaac would be misused. Maybe Jacob felt that he must protect the family because of the age of his father Isaac. We don't know. But God knows what is in a man's heart. Anyway we know that Esau was so hungry that he was willing to give or trade his birthright for a bowl of pottage or lentil soup. We see this illustrated in verses 30-32. Genesis 25:28, shows us what can happen when parents show favoritism between children.

Isaac's Lie (Chapter 26:1-17)

In this chapter, we see that the sin of the father is

repeated in the son. This is why we as parents need to realize that the statement is true. Our children many times do not do what we say as much as what we do! See Genesis 12:12 and Genesis 20:2. Isaac and Rebekkah go into the land of the Philistines. King Abimelech sees Rebekkah and desires her as his wife. Isaac, of course, like Abraham, fears for his life and tells Abimelech that Rebekkah is his sister. Like father, like son. Well, in this chapter, Isaac asked Esau to prepare wild venison before he dies and at the time of his eating, Isaac plans to pass on the family blessing to his eldest son, Esau. Rebekkah hears this and realizes that she must do something quick! She gets Jacob to kill a lamb and dress himself as Esau

and she would help Jacob disguise the meat to taste like wild venison. Rebekkah hoped, according to verse 10, that this would get Jacob the blessing instead of Esau. This scared Jacob, because he knew that he would be cursed if Isaac found out that it was Jacob instead of Esau. Rebekkah's plan was to take advantage of Isaac's blindness. According to verse 20, when Jacob brought the meat to Isaac, Isaac asked Jacob, who pretended to be Esau, how did he get the meat so fast. Jacob's response was that God gave it to him. In verse 41, Esau comes in to present his venison and finds out that he has been swindled by his younger brother Jacob. He tries to get his father to bless him but the blessing has already been given to Jacob. This angers Esau to the point that he would almost his whole life hate Jacob to the point of murdering him.

Word Study:
   A. Barren (25:21)-Without child
   B. Jostled (25:22)-To fumble around
   C. Famished (25:29)-Hungry to the point of starvation
   D. Birthright (25:31)-Inheritance
   E. Envied (26:14)-Jealous of
   F. Quiver (27:3)-Holds arrows
   G. Scarcely (27:30)-Almost gone
   H. Grudge (27:41)-To hold against someone

Notes to Consider:
There are three prayers mentioned thus far :
   A. We see Abraham's prayer for a nation.
   B. We see the servant's prayer for a bride.
   C. We see Isaac's prayer of repentance for his favoritism.

Devotional Reading: 25:20-34, 26:1-17, 27:1-47

Memory Verse: Galatians 6:7-8

LESSON 8

JACOB'S WONDERFUL NIGHTMARE

Chapter 29:1-30:24

Jacob's Dream (Chapter 28:10-22)

We see here that Jacob is running for his life from the wrath of his brother Esau. We now pick up the action with Jacob camping out under the moon of night. He is using a stone as a pillow. While asleep, Jacob has a three-fold dream. We see this dream in verses 12 and 13. Jacob's dream consisted of a ladder reaching from Heaven to Earth. There were angels going up and down the ladder from Heaven. The most wonderful thing, however, was who was at the top of the ladder. It was the Lord himself! In verse 20, Jacob asked God for two things. He asked God to be with him wherever the journey took him. Then, Jacob asked God to feed, clothe, and protect him on his travels. In verses 21-23, he promises God three things. Jacob promises God that He, the Lord, would be his God. The pillow that Jacob is lying on would be the corner-stone of the house of God. And Jacob vowed to give God a tenth of all he possessed. There is a question that arises from this passage of scripture. Does God promise to take care of his people?

63

The answer is yes! In Matthew 6:25-34, God tells us not to worry about our daily needs for God Himself has promised to take care of our needs. We must be careful though that we don't get our needs mixed up with our wants. Some people do this and wonder why they don't prosper. The answer is simple. Some people are greedy and not interested in what God's best is for their lives. We also see another principle; that God expects us to give a tenth of what we have or make to His work. It is not for God's sake, for we know that God owns everything. "Tithing" is for our sake to teach us disciple and obedience, which in the ends leads to untold blessings. Once we settle the issue of ownership, tithing will not be a problem.

Jacob's Marriages (Chapter 29:1-30)

In Genesis 29, Jacob goes to his uncle Laban to find a

wife. Jacob comes to a well to get water for his camels and himself. While at the well, Jacob meets Rachel who is Laban's youngest daughter. Jacob falls in love with Rachel and goes to Laban to get permission to marry her. Laban is a deceptive business man. In this account of love, we are going to see the tables of deception turned on Jacob. Laban tells Jacob that in order for Jacob to marry Rachel, he must be willing to work for him for seven years. To this, Jacob agrees. Love for a person can make us do abnormal things. For Jacob, it would be seven years of employment to the father of Rachel. In verse 23, we see some shocking things take place. Jacob goes through the wedding ceremony, never seeing the face of his wife.

Jacob then goes to his "honeymoon" night, only to be horrified that it is Rachel's older sister, Leah, that he married. Why did Laban do this to Jacob? The answer is in family tradition. It was customary for the oldest daughter to be married first. Laban should have made this clear, unless he did not know, or he did not care. Nevertheless, Jacob wakes up surprised. He goes to Laban  and questions Laban's integrity. Laban simply reminds Jacob of family law and tradition. Jacob, because he so loves Rachel, works another seven years for Laban. Leah was probably hated and forgotten by Jacob. Leah was not forgotten by the Lord, for she would have the most children for Jacob in the years to come. Rachel, on the other hand would have the son that would save Israel and bring into motion the family line of the Messiah.

This young man's name would be Joseph.

Jacob's Children (Genesis 29:31-30:24)

1. Listed below are the sons born of Leah and what each name means:

   A. Reuben: God has given me a son for my affliction.

   B. Simeon: God heard that I was hated.

   C. Levi: God has joined me to my husband.

   D. Judah: God is to be praised.

   E. Issachar: God has given me my hire.

   F. Zebulun: God dwells with me and rewards me.

   G. Dinah: (the only girl) God has judged me.

2. Listed below are the sons of Bilhah, Rachel's handmaid :

   A. Dan: God has heard my cry.

   B. Naphtali: God has wrestled with me.

3. Listed below are the sons of Zilphah, Leah's handmaid:

   A. Gad: God sends a troop.

   B. Asher: God is happy for me.

4. Listed below are the sons of Rachel and what each name means :

   A. Joseph: God has taken my reproach away.

   B. Benjamin (Benoni): God is God in my death.

A Note To Remember:

There are four direct prophecies concerning Christ found in the Genesis. They are as follows:

1. We see Christ as the seed of woman in Genesis 3:15

2. We see Christ as the seed of Abraham in Genesis 22:18.

3. We see Christ as the seed of Isaac in Genesis 26:4.

4. We see Christ as the seed of Jacob in Genesis 28:14

Word Study:

    A. Awesome (28:17)- Mighty

    B. Leah (29:17)- Oldest daughter of Laban

    C. Rachel (29:17)- Youngest daughter of Laban

    D. Attached (29:34)- Tied to

    E. Mandrake Plants (30:14)- An egg-type plant used for medicine

Basic Truths:

1. We can't run forever from ourselves and from God.

2. We cannot beat God.

3. Sometimes God hurts us to mold us.

4. We reap what we sow.

5. Favoritism cause jealousy.

Memory Verse: Matthew 6:25-26

JACOB MEETS HIS MATCH

Chapter 30:25-36:43

Jacob Leaves His Father-in-law (Genesis 30:25-31:55). It comes time for Jacob to leave his father-in-law, Laban. However, Laban does not want to let go of Jacob. God was blessing Jacob, and Laban had become a recipient of these blessings. Laban knew that as long as God blessed Jacob, he too would be blessed. Jacob stayed another seven years and raised livestock. During this time, God blessed Jacob's flocks in that they grew stronger and stronger, while Laban's grew weaker. During Jacob's employment with Laban, Laban changed Jacob's wages ten times. This shows how crooked Laban was. But Jacob kept working, and God kept blessing. It came time for Jacob to leave Laban. How Jacob left could be scrutinized, for he left without talking to Laban. When Jacob and his family left, Rachel stole some graven images of worship. This of course would cause problems later down the road. Why did Rachel take these graven images? There are three possible answers. First, these graven idols would guarantee good luck. Secondly, these images guaranteed Jacob's slavery and tie to Rachel's family. Thirdly, these images would still in some sense be a security, upon which she depended for spiritual matters. It is so important to make sure that the person whom we marry is spiritually equal with us in their beliefs. Laban comes, in verses 34 and 35, to find his gods have "walked" away. But we reap what we sow. If Laban had sent Jacob away, it would have probably been empty handed and poor.

Jacob Prepares to Meet Esau (32:1-21)

There comes a time when, even when we make things right, we still reap the bitter fruit of restitution and making amends. In these verses, Jacob receives word that his older brother Esau is coming to see him. Jacob panics and still tries to make up his own plans. First, Jacob sends a message to see if Esau is still angry. Jacob gets news that Esau is coming with 400 men. This scares Jacob. He does three things to prepare for Esau's coming. First, He divides his family and flocks into two groups, so that if Esau attacks one group, the other might escape. Secondly, Jacob appeals to God for help on the basis of the promises God had made to him. Lastly, Jacob sent generous gifts to Esau, in the hope that he might appease him and cool him down.

Jacob Wrestles With God (32:22-32)

There are two theories here as to who Jacob is wrestling. Some think it is the Lord Jesus Christ, and others think it is an angel such as Michael or Gabriel. We do have a clue as to who it is in verse 28. Jacob calls the place where he wrestled the man,"Peniel." Peniel means "face to face with God." In verse 25, Jacob wrestles with a man until almost day break. At the end, the opponent touches the thigh of Jacob, and Jacob's thigh comes out of joint. Now, the "runner"was helpless. No more could he run from his

problems. He would now have to stand and face them. In verse 28, something else happens. Jacob's name is changed to Israel. Jacob's name had meant "supplanter or deceiver." It would now mean "Prince." God had to meet Jacob and break him to make him new! Jacob would emerge a new person ready to face the challenges that lie ahead. It is great to know that when we come to the end of ourselves and meet Jesus, he changes us and gives us His strength for the life ahead of us. This is true salvation and transformation.

Jacob Meets Esau (33:1-20)

When we give in and let God take control, God can change another person's heart. This is what happens to Esau. When the two brothers meet, Esau runs to Jacob and embraces him, and then kisses his brother. In verse 9, Esau turns down the gifts of Jacob, because God had

blessed Esau so much, that Esau did not need the gifts of Jacob. According to Genesis 27:41-45, Esau had time to sit down and think about what had happened, and realized that this was God's will.

Jacob Returns to Bethel (35:1-15)

He we see an example of Proverbs 22:6. If we train up a child in the way that he or she should go, they will not depart, but they will return. In verse 2, God tells Jacob to return to Bethel. Bethel means "House of God." If in life there is any doubt about what to do, we as parents should teach our kids that God's house is still the place to go to get help! Before Jacob can return, God tells him that there are some things that Jacob must do. He would need to get rid of his false gods. He would need to be purified. Lastly, He would need to change his clothes. In verse 6, Jacob builds an altar to worship God. After this, God promises to bless and multiply Jacob's family. God promises to fulfill through Jacob the promise He had made to Abraham and Isaac.

Word Study:

1. Divination (30:27)-To discern the future by witchcraft.
2. Accumulating (31:10)- Gaining things.
3. Shear (31:19)- To cut the hair of sheep.
4. Pacify (32:20)- To please for a while.
5. Ford (32:22)- A small narrow strip of land over a river.
6. Defiled (34:5)- Contaminated.
7. Stench (34:30)- To stink.

Devotional Reading: Genesis 30:25-34:31

Memory Verses: Proverbs 16:7-9

LESSON 10

THE COST OF HAVING A VISION

Genesis 37, 39

Joseph's Dreams (Genesis 37:1-11)

In this chapter we once again see what favoritism can do to a family and its siblings. It can cause jealousy and bitterness. It is hard though sometimes for a parent not to show favoritism, especially when there is one child that obeys and the other one does not. This is why parenting can be so challenging sometimes. In verse 2, we see that Joseph was telling his father of his brothers' wrongdoing. Some Bible teachers believe that Joseph was being a "tattle-tell." However, we teach our kids not to lie when asked to tell the truth. This caused the brothers to hate Joseph. Another thing that put Joseph in bad light with his brothers was the fact that they saw how much Jacob loved Joseph. Jacob loved Joseph because he was the only son at this time of his wife, Rachel. Benjamin would later come into the household from Rachel. This latter birth would take her life. To show his love for Joseph, Jacob would give Joseph a coat of many colors. This was an important sign of affection for it would, in a way, transfer power of leadership from the father to the son, or supposedly the eldest son. In this case, it would go to Joseph. This would cause the brothers to hate Joseph more!

To make matters worse, Joseph would have two dreams from verses 7-9, that would put his whole household at the feet of Joseph. The first dream was of stalks of wheat (sheaves) bowing down to Joseph's stalk. The second dream would add his mom and dad in that the Sun, Moon, and Stars would bow down to Joseph. Jacob kept all this according to verse 11 to himself.

This, of course, would be the "straw that would break the camel's back." This would cause the death of Joseph, or would it?

Joseph's Slavery (Chapter 37:12-36)

In verse 18, the brothers see Joseph from afar and plot to kill him. The plan was to kill Joseph and put his body in an abandoned well or pit. Then the brothers would tell Jacob that a wild beast had eaten Joseph. Reuben over hears this and decides that he was going to put a stop to this. He probably wanted to scare Joseph and then let him go later. Reuben thus talked the brothers into just putting Joseph into the pit. Reuben was going to come back and let Joseph out. The brothers agreed and put Joseph in a pit. While Reuben is gone, Judah comes up with another plan when he sees a caravan coming. He convinces the brothers to sell Joseph as a slave for twenty pieces of silver. So Joseph would become a slave to a group of Ishmaelites on their way to Egypt.

There would be one problem though, how would they explain Joseph's disappearance to their dad? To cover up their crime, the brothers decided to kill a goat and take its blood and put it on Joseph's coat. They would then take it to their dad, Jacob, and say that a wild beast had slain and eaten Joseph. The Bible then records for us Jacob's response when he was told Joseph was dead. He tore his clothes and put on sackcloth, and mourned for many days. Verse 35 tells us that the family tried to comfort Jacob. Later on, Joseph would travel down life's road that would lead to the greatest test of his life. It would be the road to greatness. The Ishmaelites  would go to Egypt and sell Joseph to Pharaoh's personal body guard. This great man was known as Potiphar.

Joseph's Temptation (Chapter 39)

Sometimes God has to get us away from family and the familiar surrounding of home to build into us what he needs for us to be, his instrument. It is very crucial at this time, for we can either become stronger or weaker. Verse two of this chapter shows us that it is not the things in life that make or brake us, it is our attitude that does this. Joseph decided that he would love and follow the Lord. Potiphar quickly found out that Joseph had God's favor on his life. It came a time when Potiphar so trusted

Joseph that he put him in charge of the very things that Potiphar was accountable for. Potiphar so trusted Joseph that he gave Joseph rule over his own house. But as Satan is, Satan would tempt Joseph by the only thing that Joseph did not have control over and that was Potiphar's wife. According to verse 7, Potiphar's wife would try for several days to get Joseph to commit immorality with her. Joseph refused. There were two reasons given in verse 9. Joseph had made up his mind that he would not wrong his master. Joseph would not sin against God. Joseph considers who he was. He considers how bad sin was. He considers who he was sinning against. Well, the old adage is true "there is nothing more worse than a woman spurned!" Potiphar's wife decides that since Joseph will not commit immorality with her, accusing him of this would be the next best thing.

According to verse 14-15, she makes us a story accusing Joseph of trying to take advantage of her while her help is out. She screams to make it appear that something is wrong. Then lastly, she grabs his cloak when he tries to run so that she can have proof that Joseph was there with her. After all, who is going to doubt Potiphar's wife? When Potiphar finds out, he puts Joseph into prison. But once again God was with Joseph. While in prison, Joseph found favor with the head of the prison and it is not long before Joseph is running the prison, according to verse 22.

NOTES TO REMEMBER:

A. Things that led to Joseph being hated by his brothers:
Chapter 37
> 1. He was a teller of the truth. 2b
> 2. He only told the facts about things. 2b
> 3. He was a "daddy's" boy. 3a
> 4. He was given a coat from daddy. 3b
> 5. He was a dreamer of dreams. 5
> 6. He was an interpreter of dreams. 8

B. "One sin leads to another; sin builds upon sin."

We see that in this chapter, there is a progression to sin. In verse four, we see that the brothers hated Joseph or disliked the way he acted. In verse 5, the hatred gets more intense. The Bible says that the brothers hated him more or even more, despised him. In verse 8, they went further in their hatred. They hated Joseph more and even to the point that they wanted Joseph out of the way. In verse 11, we see jealousy. In verse 18, we see that the brothers then decided to do bodily harm. Verse 20 we see the brothers of Joseph scheming to harm Joseph. In verse 27 we see the final act of selling Joseph their own brother and not feeling any remorse for doing so.

C. Ten Biblical Truths to consider when being tempted.
> 1. When Should one abstain? I Corinthians 6:12
> 2. Will it bring Glory to God? I Corinthians 10:31

3. Will it harm the body? I Corinthians 6:18

4. Will it harm my life testimony? Matthew 5:13-16

5. Is it a stumbling block to others? I Corinthians 8:9

6. Is it a weight in my life? Hebrews 12:1

7. Can we do it in Jesus' name? Colossians 3:17-23

8. Can we pray for God's guidance? Proverbs 10:22

9. Does it seem wrong or have a bad name? I Thessalonians 5:22

10. Is it of the world? I John 2:15-17

Word Study:

A. Ornamented (37:3)-Decorated

B. Binding (37:7)-It must be kept and honored.

C. Sheaves (37:7)-Barley bails.

D. Cisterns (37:19)-Water jugs.

E. Attendant (39:4)-One who attends to others.

F. Entrusted (39:8)-Something trusted to someone care.

G. Confined (39:20)-Not being able to move about.

Devotional Reading: Genesis 37 & 39

Memory Verses: I Corinthians 6:12, 10:31, 6:19-20

LESSON 7

THE DREAM INTERPRETER

Genesis 40-44

Joseph Interprets Dreams While in Prison
(Genesis 40-41)

Joseph is thrown in prison which was most likely an answer to the grace of God. In those days, rape or immorality with another man's wife was considered a punishable act of death. Instead Joseph was put in prison. Could it be that Potiphar knew that Joseph was innocent? Was it that Potiphar just needed to save face in front of his society? These questions are not really answered in the Bible. According to verses 1-3, we see the two chief members of Pharaoh's staff in jail with Joseph. One staff member was a butler and the other the chief baker. While in prison each of these men bring a dream to Joseph and Joseph interprets the dream. Joseph of course uses his circumstances to point people to God.

This situation answers the question of "What do I do when I'm in a place that I don't believe God would have me in?" We see what Joseph did. He used his circumstance for the furthering of God's kingdom. Joseph had learned that his life would take different directions but, that this was an opportunity to point others to the Lord and that instead of being disgruntled with the place we are in, we need to see it as a "divine" opportunity to serve the God of Heaven and be a witness of the grace of God.

Joseph interprets the Butler's dream first. In verses 9-11, the dream had to do with vines that yielded wine. Joseph's interpretation was that in three days Pharaoh will lift the Butler to his original staff position. Joseph also interpreted the dream of the chief Baker. In verses 16 and 17 this dream had to do with baked bread. In verses 18-19, this dream has an unusual turn in that the birds come and eat the bread. This dream said that in three days the Baker would be executed by Pharaoh. The Baker would be hung on a tree. This would happen on Pharaoh's birthday of all days according to verse 20. Joseph had asked these men, especially the Butler to remember him. The Butler forgot Joseph.

In Chapter 41, however, Pharaoh had several dreams that bothered him. His first dream consisted of 7 cows that were skinny and sickly eating 7 fat, healthy cows. This happens in verse 4. The second dream consisted of 7 thin heads of corn swallowing up 7 fat, full stalks of corn. Pharaoh summons his magicians to try and interpret the dreams and they could not. Finally the Chief Butler remembers Joseph. This is a good place to remind us to be a blessing to everyone we meet no matter how we are treated. The person that you help could one day be a huge blessing to you when you need it the most. Joseph is brought to Pharaoh and he hears Pharaoh recite the dreams. Joseph interprets the dreams. The second part of the dream represented that Egypt would have seven years of plenty. This was represented by the fat cows and the fat corn stalks. These seven years would be quickly eaten by seven years of famine. These years were represented by the skinny cows and thin ears of corn. After this happens there would be no food in Egypt at all. What was Pharaoh to do? In verse 36, Joseph becomes a "Problem Solver." The world today like the world of yesteryear is still looking for "Problem Solvers" and not "Problem Makers." Joseph suggests in verse 36 that Pharaoh appoint someone he trusted to oversee the project of gathering all they could for seven years and then the distribution of food during the seven years of famine. Well, according to verse 38 and 39 Joseph is appointed to the job of overseeing this food project. But why did Pharaoh trust a man he did not know? The Bible says that Pharaoh saw that the Spirit of the Lord was on Joseph. He saw the maturity of Joseph in that Joseph was wise and discreet. Joseph was placed Second in command only to Pharaoh himself. We see this in verse 43. While in Egypt, Joseph marries and has two sons and he calls one Manasseh (God has made me forget my troubles), and the other son is called Ephraim (God had made me fruitful in my affliction). Thus we see that Joseph's attitude made the difference. We see here that our circumstances have nothing to do with our attitude, for attitude is a choice! We can choose to become bitter at what comes our way or we can choose to let it make us wiser and stronger in character as a person. We can choose to let God make it better.

Joseph's Brothers Visits. (Chapter 42-44)

"To Forgive or not to Forgive."

The First Visit (Chapter 42)

On the first visit the youngest brother named Benjamin did not go. The reason had to be that Jacob had already lost one son of Rachel. Jacob did not want to lose another and only son of his wife Rachel. When the brothers arrived in Egypt, Joseph saw them. He entertained them but according to verse eight they did not recognize Joseph. This was probably due to the make-up and garb of that day. Joseph decides to use this disguise to test his brothers. In verse 9 of this chapter, Joseph accuses his brothers of being spies. He then puts them to the test by telling them to prove that they are not spies. The test was to bring their youngest brother back with them to get food. All of this communication was done through an interpreter. The brothers go back and get Benjamin. To make sure that they come back Joseph keeps Simeon in prison. In verse 25, Joseph does three things for his brothers on their way out. Joseph has each man's bag filled with grain. Joseph puts each man's money back in their sacks. Lastly, Joseph added provisions for each man. When the brothers got home they relayed the message to Jacob, that Simeon was in jail and that they had to bring Benjamin back with them to get Simeon out of prison. Jacob was totally against this. To add to this they had found all the money and extra provisions in their sacks and this scared them even more thinking that Joseph would come after them thinking that they had stolen these things!

The Second Visit (Chapter 42 and 44)

We pick up with chapter 43 and verse 3 with Judah protesting going back to Egypt. The reason for his protest was that they had already lost Joseph and Judah felt that they were going to lose Benjamin. After all, Joseph had told them not to come back without Benjamin anyway. Judah promises to be the one blamed if the brothers do not return with Benjamin. The brothers journey to Egypt one more time. This time it is a trip of mercy. In verse 16, the brothers are invited to eat with Joseph. During the supper, Joseph asked if Jacob was doing well and is Jacob even alive. As all this information is being revealed, Joseph leaves the room for he wants to so badly tell his brothers that he is alive and in their presence. We notice that the brothers ate at another table according to verse 32. Why was this? The answer is that it was forbidden for Egyptians to eat with lower levels of society. The Hebrews were considered in this category. Joseph according to verse 33 had his brothers seated from oldest to the youngest. When it came time for the brothers to leave, in chapter 44 and verses 1-2, Joseph had his steward fill the men's sacks with as much corn as they could carry. The steward was to put each man's money back in his sack. Then the steward was to put Joseph's cup in the mouth of the youngest one's sack along with money for his corn. In chapter 43 and verse 34, the steward was to put five times the amount of corn in Benjamin's bags. The next things that the steward was to do was to send the brothers on their way and then in a little while chase them and when he overtook the brothers, the steward was to accuse them of stealing, according to chapter 44:4.

Verse 9 of chapter 44 tells us that two things could happen to a thief. The person whose sack it was found could die. The rest of the brothers could become slaves. According to verse 12, the cup of Joseph was found in Benjamin's bag. The brothers are in real trouble now. What would they do? In verse 20, Judah offers a plea. Judah says " We have an old father, and Benjamin was born to Jacob in his old age. His brother, (speaking of Joseph) is dead, and he is the only one of his mother's sons alive." Judah went on to tell that Jacob greatly loved Benjamin and that according to verse 29, if Benjamin died, it would be more than Jacob could bear. This would kill Jacob. At this moment it had come full circle of how much hurt had been caused because of their insecurity and jealousy against Joseph. God has a way of allowing things to come full circle to get our attention!

Word Study:

A. Custody-(40:3)-Possession of something.

B. Dejected-(40:6)-A feeling of rejection.

C. Forcibly-(40:15)-To do something by force.

D. Gaunt-(41:3)-To be skinny or lacking.

E. Ravage-(41:30)-To destroy or take advantage of.

F. Discerning-(41:39)-To be able to judge a matter.

G. "Signet Ring"- (41:42)-Symbol of authority and power.

H. Verified-(42:20)-to make sure and true.

I. Deprived-(42:20)-To do without.

J. Entrust-(42:37)-To put into the trust of.

K. Solemnly-(43:3)-To be serious about.

L. Bereaved-(43:14)-To hurt because of a loss.

M. Divination-(44:5)-To use objects to determine the future.

Devotional Reading: Genesis 40-44

Memory Verses: Romans 12:17-21

WHEN FORGIVENESS HURTS

Genesis 45-50

Joseph Reveals Himself (Chapter 45)

Joseph apparently could not bear his brothers not knowing it was he. In verse 3 of chapter 45, Joseph reveals himself to his brothers. Their reaction was one of amazement and confusion. They were greatly troubled and upset, probably ashamed of themselves. But in verse 5, Joseph reminds and assures them that this was done by God to save many people. In verse 7, he tells his brothers that God sent him to Egypt to preserve for them a posterity on the earth and to save their lives

by a great deliverance. In verse 9, before Joseph allows his brothers to leave for home, he tells his brothers to tell Jacob that he is alive and well. He instructs his brothers to bring his father to Egypt. The brothers return home and share the good news, and in verse 26, we see that Jacob doubted the news. But, when Jacob saw the wagons, he knew that God had heard his cry of remorse.

Joseph's Family in Egypt (Chapters 46-50)

God comes to Jacob, in verses 2 and 3, and tells Jacob to go to Egypt. When Jacob saw Joseph, he knew that now it was alright to die in peace. In chapter 47, Jacob and his

family are given the land of Goshen. Goshen was a well-watered valley. In verses 16-19, Joseph gathered up all of the money in the land and stored it in Pharaoh's palace. Then, when famine came, Joseph gave the people three different payment options in order for them to be able to buy food:

1). They could purchase food with their livestock.

2). They could serve Pharaoh by farming the land of Pharaoh.

3).They could give to Pharaoh one-fifth of their land for his own possession. They would then be able to keep four-fifths of the land for themselves. Joseph would give each farmer corn seed, and he could grow corn to give back to Pharaoh in payment for bread. The Hebrews, during this time, prospered and grew in number according to verse 27. Before Jacob dies, he makes Joseph promise to bury him with his fathers in Canaan. After this, Jacob then blesses the sons of Joseph. Joseph had two sons. This small portion of scripture shows the fore-sight of God. When Jacob goes to bless the two boys, he blesses the youngest over the oldest. Why? These verses reveal to us that the youngest would become many nations, and that the oldest would not.

As parents, we must let God work in the lives of our children as He sees fit. If we have given our children to God, then we must believe that Proverbs 22:6 will work. It says in this verse the if a parent trains up a child in the way that he should go, then the parent is assured that when that child is old, he/she will not depart from it. Our teaching and modeling as a parent of the things of God will always be a reminder of where that child needs to be. This is a wonderful thought to remember!

In chapter 49 of Genesis, Jacob then blesses his own sons. They are broken down as follows:

A. **Leah's Children** (1-15) :
  1. Reuben (3-5)—The tribe of Reuben was a tribe of good intentions, but low on productivity. Reuben was full of good ideas, but was slow on follow-through. The symbol of this tribe was "over-flowing pot." They would have no kings, princes or real leadership (Judges 5:15, 16; I Chronicles 5:1)
  2. Simeon and Levi (5-7)—These two tribes were comrades in murder! Remember the massacre in Shechem. Their symbol would be that of instruments of cruelty such as axe or sword. These two tribes were either dis-inherited or separated unto the Lord. Simeon's tribe was given an inheritance within the tribe of Judah (Joshua 19:1; I Chronicles 4:39-43). Levi became the priestly tribe with no homeland of their own (Joshua 21:1-3).
  3. Judah (8-12)—This tribe became the "prince" among tribes. It's symbol was the Lion. Through this tribe the Messiah would come.

4. Zebulun and Issachar (13-15)—These two tribes were known as the "twin" tribes. They were always together. They were the serving tribes. Zebulun's symbol was the ship, and Issachar's symbol was the donkey. Zebulun had contact with the people of Zidon. These people we know today as the Phoenicians. Issachar was the submissive tribe. They were always willing to serve others.

B. **The Concubine Children** (16-21) :

1. Dan (16-18)—Dan was a fierce tribe. They would fight without warning (Judges 18). Their symbol was that of an Eagle. Dan was removed from the list of tribes in Revelation 7:4-8. They were guilty of blaspheming God on many occasions (Leviticus 24:11; Judges 18; I Kings 12:28-29).

2. Gad (19)—Gad was the military tribe. Their symbol was that of a soldier.

3. Asher (20)—The tribe of Asher were the cooks. Their symbol was that of a basket of fruit, or "Horn of Plenty." There are no famous deeds about this tribe. The last descendant of this tribe was Anna (Luke 2:36).

4. Naphtali (21)—Naphtali was the counseling tribe, or the singers of the group. Their symbol was the deer and the harp.

C. **The Children of Rachel** (22-27) :

    1. Joseph (22-26)—This tribe was the harvesting tribe. Their symbol was the "Big Stone."

    2. Benjamin (27)—This was a nomadic, barbaric tribe. They were always seeking new prey. Their symbol was a hunting wolf. King Saul (I Samuel 9:1-2), and the apostle Paul (Romans 11:1), were Benjaminites.

Joseph's Last Days (Chapter 50)

There was a little worry in the camp of Jacob at the coming of his death. According to verse 15, the brothers of Joseph worried about him retaliating against them at their father's death. In verse 17, the brothers recite to Joseph the instructions that Jacob had left for Joseph. Jacob asked Joseph to forgive the brothers their transgression and the sin they committed in selling Joseph to the Ishmaelites. Jacob asked Joseph to forgive the transgressions of the servants of the Lord of his father. In verses 19-21, we see some of the greatest words ever penned on forgiveness, and why God allows suffering. Joseph looks at his brothers and instructs them to not be afraid. He asks a question, "Am I in the place of God?" This reminds us that it is our creator that calls the order of our lives and not us. Joseph finishes with this statement of truth and wisdom: "You intended to kill me, but God intended it for good to accomplish what is now being done, the salvation of many people. I will provide for you and your children." This great book closes with the death of Joseph at the age of 110.

Word Study:

A. Remnant (45:7)—The last remaining family.

B. Destitute (45:11)—Lacking in material and physical possessions.

C. Detestable (46:34)- Hated very much.

D. Pilgrimage (47:9)—A religious journey

E. Desolate (47:19)—Left totally empty.

F. Allotment (47:22)—A portion given out.

G. Turbulent (49:4)—Troublesome

I. Hamstrung (49:6)—To make one lame.

J. Delicacies (49:20)—Sweet desserts.

K. Embalm (50:2)—To preserve.

L. Dignitaries (50:7)—Government Officials.

Joseph a Type of Christ:

A. *Unger's Bible Handbook* Page 78

   1. Both were special objects of a father's love (Gen. 37:3; Mt. 3:17; Jn. 3:35).

   2. Both were hated and rejected by their brethren (Gen. 37:4; Jn. 15:25).

   3. Both made unusual predictions which were rejected by their brothers.

   4. In both cases, brothers conspired to kill them (Gen. 37:18; Mt. 26:3-4).

   5. Joseph was, in intent and figure, put to death by

his brothers. Christ was also.

6. Both became a "savior" among the Gentiles and acquired a Gentile "Bride."

7. As Joseph brought his brothers to himself, and afterwards forgave them, so will Christ at his second coming do likewise. Christ will thus become the "Bride Groom."

B. *Gleanings in Genesis* (pages 344-352)

1. The meaning of his name:

A. Joseph and Zaphnathpaaneah (41:45)

Joseph = Hebrew name.

Zaphnathpaaneah = Egyptian name.

B. Jesus and Christ

Jesus = His human name

Christ = His divine name.

2. By occupation, Joseph was a shepherd, "feeding the flock."

3. His opposition to wickedness:

A. Joseph was a " sin - bearer."

B. John 7:7

4. His Father's love:

A. Jacob loved Joseph.

B. God loves Christ.

(Mt. 3:17; 17:5; John 10:17)

5. His relation to his father's age:

A. Joseph was the "son of Jacob's old age."

    B. Jesus Christ is the Son of God's eternity! (John 1:1; 17:5)

6. His coat of many colors:
    A. Joseph's coat was a coat of authority (Judges 5:30; II Samuel 13:18)
    B. Christ was set apart from, and elevated above, all others (John 12 & 13).

7. The hatred of his brothers:
    A. "They hated him and could not speak peaceably to him."
    B. "If any man love not the Lord Jesus Christ, let him be accursed!"

8. Joseph is hated because of his dreams:
    A. Twofold occasion for their hatefulness:
      1) They hated Joseph's dreams.
      2) They hated him because of his predictions.
    B. Twofold occasion for hatred toward Christ:
      1) Hated because He is the Son of God (John 5:18).
      2) Hated because of his predictions (John 6:41).

9. Joseph was to enjoy a remarkable future:
    A. His dreams were announcements of his future

       authority and leadership.

   B.   A remarkable future was promised to the one who first appeared in heaven and earth (Isaiah 9:6-7; Luke 1:31-33).

10. Joseph was sold by his brothers:

     A. They were jealous of him.

      B. Christ was "envied" by those who were his brethren, according to the flesh.

Devotional Reading: Genesis 45:1 - 46:7; 47:13 - 31; 48:1 - 49:28; 50:15 - 26

Memory Verses: Genesis 50:20; Romans 8:28

INTRODUCTION TO EXODUS

The author of Exodus is Moses. The life of Moses was divided into three periods of 40 years each. There were forty years in Egypt as the son of Pharaoh's daughter (Exodus 2:1-12). Here, Moses thought he was a "Prince." There were forty years in the wilderness of Midian (Exodus 2:15 - 4:19). Here, Moses was learning that he was a "shepherd." Then lastly, Moses spent forty years from Egypt to the brink of the promised land (Exodus 4:20 -Deuteronomy 34). "He was discovering what God could do with a servant." Evidence found from this book itself leads one to the conclusion that the author was a wealthy, educated man. This man was a long-time resident of Egypt. He was a leader of the Exodus. This book was written from Mount Sinai in the Arabian peninsula between 1445 to 1400 B.C.

God's role in this book would be one of guidance and the provider of the laws governing God's nation. God's command was "Come out from among them!" The key verse is Exodus 12:23 which states: "For the Lord will pass through to smite the Egyptians: and when he seeth the blood upon the lintel, and on the two side posts, the Lord will pass over the door, and will not suffer the destroyer to come in unto your houses to smite you."This book tells of the redeeming work of a sovereign God in rescuing man from his bondage of sin. The key word of this book is Exit. **The outline is as follows:**

I.   Israel in Egypt (Bondage) (Chapters 1 - 12)

II. Israel in the wilderness (Deliverance) (Chapters 13 - 18)

III. Israel at Mt. Sinai (Instruction) (Chapters 19 - 40)

Notes to Remember about the book of Exodus are;

A. Overview of the Book:

The people are in bondage in chapters 1 and 2 showing the burdensome condition of the people of God. In chapters 3 - 15:21, we see the redemption of God coming down a river in a basket to deliver Israel. We then see the education of the people as they travel in the wilderness to Mt Sinai in chapters 15:22 - 19:25. This was a spiritual education to get them to totally rely upon God. In chapter 20 - 23, we see the consecration (setting apart). The redeemed must do the work of the redeemer, and must <u>consecrate</u> themselves to His will. Israel is then taught to worship God in God's own unique and holy way (Ex. 24 - 40).

B. "Exodus begins in darkness and gloom, yet ends in glory; it commences by telling how God came down in grace to deliver an enslaved people, and ends by declaring how God came down in glory to dwell in the midst of a redeemed people."

C. Exodus deals with three major subjects: Slavery to Egypt, Salvation from Egypt, and Submission to the God of Israel.

Part III

BONDAGE

EXODUS 1-12

LESSON 1

WHAT DOES FAITH
AND TRUST LOOK LIKE?

Exodus 1-4

Moses' Background (Chapters 1 and 2)

This book begins with a new Pharaoh who did not know the God of Israel. During this time the children of Israel were growing by leaps and bounds. God began to bless the birth rate of the Hebrew women. This greatly disturbed and frightened Pharaoh. Pharaoh was worried about the possibility of the Hebrews joining with their enemies and then overrunning the nation of Egypt. In verse 16, Pharaoh orders the midwives to kill the male babies as soon as they are born. The midwives were to take the male Hebrew babies and throw them into the Nile River. There was however one Hebrew woman from the tribe of Levi that hid her baby. The baby's name was Moses. She hid Moses in some bulrushes next to the Nile River. The mother of Moses put him in a basket and hid the basket and baby in the bulrushes. The basket would then make its way down the river into the personal presence of Pharaoh's daughter. Miriam, Moses' sister, monitored this basket all the way down to its predetermined resting place. The Bible tells us that Pharaoh's daughter basically fell in love with the baby. She would soon call this baby Moses. Moses means, "drawn from water." Moses grows up in the finest and most influential households of his day. He is the son of Pharaoh! This would

automatically assure Moses of the finest training and education afforded in that day. This would assure Moses of a secure future as the next Pharaoh. Moses would be set the rest of his life.

According to verse 11, Moses is out and about and sees an Egyptian taskmaster beating a Hebrew slave. He quickly looks to see if any one is looking and kills the taskmaster with his own hands. Moses quickly buries the taskmaster in the sands and goes to the palace. The next day (according to verse 13 of chapter 2), Moses sees two Hebrew brothers fighting, and he stopped and told them to stop fighting. Their reply was horrifying to Moses. In verse fourteen, one of the Jews stated the following to Moses;

"Who made you prince over us? We saw what you did to that Egyptian taskmaster, and we know where you buried him!" This caused Moses to panic and flee from the presence of the Pharaoh of Egypt. Moses knew that it would be just a matter of time before others knew of this incident. So Moses fled to the wilderness plains of

Midian. Moses was truly a special man. Pharaoh's daughter could have had Moses killed as a baby, but the Bible tells us that she had compassion on him. She knew that God had spared Moses from the animals and waves of the Nile River.

However, special preeminence does not mean that we can take matters into our own hands, even though we must take responsibility for our own actions. God does not look at our status in life to discipline us because of disobedience. Moses got ahead of his position and now had to run for his life. Even if our heart is in the right place, we can still disobey God by getting ahead of His plan.

Moses' Calling (Chapters 3-4)

While in the desert plains of Midian, Moses met a Midianite who would later turn out to be a huge blessing to him. This man named Jethro would later become the father-in-law of Moses. According to verse 3 of chapter 3, Moses has an encounter with Jehovah God! Sometimes God has to get us alone in a desolate place so that He is all that we can see and hear. God appears and shows up in some of the most unusual ways. In these verses, God shows up in the form of a "burning bush." The

unique thing about this bush is that it did not burn up! In verse 5, God tells Moses to take off his shoes, for the place where He is standing is holy ground! We need to be reminded that God lives in us as Christians by the Holy Spirit. This means that every where we are standing is "holy ground!" Why? If God is there, (and He is through the Holy Spirit), the place is holy unto the Lord. Be careful where you stand! While Moses is standing in this holy place, God reveals His plan for him. Sometimes God does not reveal his plans to us until we become serious about His will for our lives. God wants to entrust us with His work. Can He trust us?

In verses 11 through chapter 4:10, Moses offers up four excuses to God as to why he cannot deliver the children of Israel from Egypt. In chapter 3:11, Moses says, "I'm a failure." In verse 13, Moses says, "I have nothing to say." In chapter 4:1, Moses says, "I have no power or authority." In verse 10, Moses says, "I cannot speak." But now look at God's answers. In Chapter 3:12, God says, "When God is with you, you're a success!" In verses 14-22, God says, "When I am with you, you'll have plenty to say!" In chapter 4:2-9, God says, "When I am with you, you will have my authority and power!" God then gave Moses three object lessons to show that Moses would have the authority of God. His rod would turn into a snake. His hand would turn into leprosy. His rod would turn the rivers into blood. In chapter 4:11-12, God finalizes His rebuttal to Moses' excuses. "Who made your mouth?" In verse 14 of chapter 4, God would get Aaron, Moses' brother to be his "Mouth."

A good principle to remember here is this; God does not accept our excuses, but, He does provide for our weaknesses! Where God leads, God most certainly will provide. God will also allow our resolve to be tested. According to verse 21, God would allow Pharaoh's heart to become hard. This would come down (according to verse 23) to the death of the first-born of the land of Egypt.

Word Study:

A. Shrewdly (1:10)- Clever and cunning

B. Oppress (1:11)- To inflict hardship and pain.

C. Ruthlessly (1:13)- To act without mercy.

D. Vigorous (1:19)- To work hard.

E. Papyrus (2:3)- Paper made from flax and reeds.

F. Spacious (3:8)- Plenty of room

G. Plunder (3:22)- To destroy and mess up.

H. Eloquent(4:10)- To speak with clarity.

Devotional Reading: Exodus 1-4

Memory Verses: Hebrews 11:23-26

FAITH AND OBEDIENCE TESTED

Exodus 5:1-7:13

Moses First Visit With Pharaoh (5:1-7:7)

When Moses went back to Egypt, he had to put behind his past. If we are going to run the race that God has set before us, we must be willing to put behind us the failures of the past. The past will only rob you of the future. Moses had to put this behind him to be able to face Pharaoh. Remember that Moses had murdered an Egyptian taskmaster and buried him in the sand. Moses was possibly facing murder charges as well. When Moses faces Pharaoh, he faces a man who does not know the God of Jacob. We know this to be true by Pharaoh's response in verse 2. Pharaoh asks, " Who is the Lord, that I should obey him?" Pharaoh further states that he does not know the Lord and that he would not let

Israel go. In verse 3, Moses then asks Pharaoh to allow the people of God to go three days into the wilderness to worship their God, Jehovah. To this, Pharaoh's answer is no! To make things worse, Pharaoh makes a new order for the

nation of Israel. In verses 6-9, Pharaoh states that Israel will no longer enjoy their help from Egypt. They would

no longer get supplied with straw for their bricks. Israel would now have to get their own straw. Israel would also be expected to make the same number of bricks as before. Pharaoh stated that Israel was a lazy nation, and now they would have to work hard for their keep. In verse 17, the Israeli foremen were beaten by the taskmasters for not making the people work harder. When things get harder, we can do one of two things. We can either praise God and meet the demand, or we can get bitter and play the blame game. The Israeli foremen blamed Moses for this hardship. Moses goes to God and

blames Him. Notice the response of God in Exodus 6:6-8. In these verses, God reminds Moses that He will take care of Israel and guide them. But, when some people are down and discouraged, they can't see another day as a  better day. This was Israel's response to Moses in verse 9. God would keep His promise that He had made to Abraham. God had heard the cries of His people, and now was the time to act! In chapter 7:8-13, Moses pays Pharaoh another visit. This time, God uses the rod of Aaron to demonstrate the power of God. Pharaoh, thinking he has the upper hand, calls his magicians to duplicate the same act. In verses 11 and 12, the magicians cast down their rods, and the rods turn into snakes as well. Satan always tries to duplicate God's things. But in verse 12, God shows why His power is greater than Satan's. In verse 12, Aaron's staff swallows up the magician's staffs. You would think that Pharaoh would see this and realize who he was battling against, but Pharaoh's heart becomes more hardened.

Word Study:

    A. Quota: (5:8)—A mark of accomplishment.

    B. Yoke: (6:6)—Burden of Responsibility

    C. "Faltering Lips" (6:12)—Lips less than assurance and clarity.

    D. Sorcerers (7:11)—Performers of wickedness and trickery.

Project: List on a piece of paper where you find these two phrases, starting at chapter 7 and going through chapter 11:

    "Let My People Go"

    "Pharaoh's Heart Became Hardened"

Devotional Reading: Exodus 5:1-6:12; 6:28-7:13

Memory Verses: Hebrews 11:27-29

WHAT DOES GOD DO WITH DISOBEDIENCE?

Exodus 7:14-12:36

Comfort of the Egyptians

Things start to go from bad to worse. Pharaoh deprives the Israelites of water to drink and bath. He then has the Egyptian soldiers invade the homes of the Hebrews at their will. The people of Israel then have to put up with verbal harassment from the Egyptians. Well, God hears the cries of His people and says enough is enough! One of these days God is going to say "Enough, Son, go get your children!!!" Glory to God! What a day this will be !! God will now send a series of plagues as

judgment for Pharaoh's stubbornness. God also sends these plagues as a sign to the Jews that Jehovah is in total control over the plights of men. He knows what needs to be done to set His people free. God is always on time.

The Blood: (7:14-24)

In verses 17-18, God sends His first judgment. He instructed Moses to take Aaron's rod and touch the Nile

River. All water would turn to blood. This plague would kill all fish life. It would send a bad smell because of the death contained in the water. The Egyptians would not be able to drink and take baths either. This plague would affect every water source, from the streams to the vessels that contained water in them. This plague would strike at the very heart of the existence of the Egyptians. The Nile was their source of sustaining life. They would not be able to drink and eat. It would bog down their travel.

The Frogs: (8:1-15)

In this plague, there would arise life from the Nile, but it would be in the form of millions of frogs! These amphibians would be found in the most opportune places. They would be found in the Egyptians homes, in their bedrooms. They would also be in the homes of the servants and on the people themselves as they walked. During this plague, Pharaoh called for Moses and Aaron to come before him. He instructed Moses to talk to God and make Him take away the frogs. If God would do this, Pharaoh would let the people go. These frogs were considered sacred to the Egyptians for three reasons: the frogs kept the insect population down; the frogs were sacred god's of peace; and the frogs were security against foreign enemies.

The Lice: (8:16-19) #3

There are several ideas as to what the sand brought forth that day. Some versions say that these were sand fleas. Other versions say it was gnats. The Bible says that it was lice. Whatever it was that the sand brought forth, we know that it was such a judgment that Pharaoh's magicians could not duplicate it. This was the finger of God. No man could touch this judgment.

The Flies: (8:20-32) #4

This plague was so bad that it was a constant aggravation to the Egyptians. These insects would be on the servants. They would be on the people and in their houses along with the sand when it was blown. The only area that would not be affected by this plague would be the Hebrew homes located in the land of Goshen. In verse 25 and verse 28, Pharaoh tries to make a compromise both times with Moses. One would do well to remember that God does not bargain His holiness with man or with the devil. Pharaoh tells Moses that the people could worship God in the land of Egypt. In verse 28, Pharaoh then says that they can go and worship but not too far away.

The Disease of the Cattle: (9:1-7) #5

This plague would affect the cattle of Egypt. This disease would come upon the animals to the point that it would contaminate and kill the animals. The Hebrew population once again would not be harmed.

The Incurable Boils: (9:8-12) #6

This plague would attack the human flesh to the point of deteriorating the flesh. Moses was instructed to take ashes and cast them in the wind. This would cause sores and inflammation of the skin.

The Hail from Heaven: (9:13-35) #7

Some have likened this to the final 3 years of the Tribulation Period talked about in the book of Revelation. These last four judgments would utterly desolate and destroy the Egyptian economy and spirit. God was going to send this full force of judgment so that "you may know that there is no one like me in all the earth.

And that I might show you power, and that my name might be declared throughout in all the earth." This plague would kill and maim many Egyptians and their property. At this point, Pharaoh confesses seven things to Moses. Pharaoh states, "This time I have

sinned. The Lord is righteous. I and my people are in the wrong. We have had enough. I will let you go. You don't have to stay any longer." As soon as the hail stopped, Pharaoh broke his promise.

The Locust: (10:3-20) #8

This plague would totally destroy the fields and farms of Egypt. God says that they will cover the face of the earth so that it cannot be seen. The locust will eat what little the Egyptians have left. The locusts will eat their trees. This event would make Egypt's history a tragic trail of events. At this point, all of Pharaoh's top advisors are urging him to let Israel go. This time, Pharaoh confesses that he has sinned not only against the Lord, but

against Moses and his people. He now asks that Moses and the people of Israel forgive him. He asks Moses to talk to God once more and get God to remove this plague.

The Darkness: (10:21-29)

This darkness would not be just any darkness of night. This darkness would be the darkness of Hell! There would be no light at all. No Moon! No Stars! This darkness would literally be so thick that it would be felt with a fear of being locked in a casket without air. God would shine on Israel with His light!!! At this point, God is testing Pharaoh's

promise during the locust tragedy. Pharaoh calls Moses and gives him a stern warning. He tells Moses to get out of his sight. He warns Moses that the next time Moses sees the face of Pharaoh it will be the face of death! Based on this threat, Pharaoh seals the future of his son, as well as the sons of a nation. That day, Pharaoh spoke death to his own people. But as we will see later, God is a merciful God, not willing that any perish.

The Death of the First Born Child: (11:1-10)

This chapter is a terrifying chapter, for we see the angel of death that we must all meet. Every first born child of Egypt will die! From the first born of Pharaoh to the first born child of the maid-servant girl. All the first born of the beasts will die as well. There will be crying throughout all Egypt. This would bring Pharaoh to his knees. God would spare his own. There would have to be a sacrifice. Someone would have to pay!!!

The Passover: (12:1-36)

The sacrifice would have to be a lamb old enough, without blemish. They could not take them from the beasts or goats. Once the lamb was slain, the blood had to be put on the side post and over the top lentil post of each house. Exodus 12:37 tells us that 600,000 lambs were killed that day. After they sacrificed the lambs, the Hebrews were to take the lambs and cook the meat over an open fire along with bitter herbs and bread made without yeast.

This is an Old Testament foreshadow of what would take place at the cross of Calvary thousands of years later. They were not to eat the meat raw or soak it in water. They were to eat it in the morning. They were to eat it with their garments tucked into their waste bands. They were to have their shoes on. They were to have their staffs in their hands. They were to eat it in haste. In verse 13, we see that the blood would be a payment or covering for their household's sin. In verse 31-32, Pharaoh tells Moses

to go far away from Egypt. He lets them go to serve their God as requested. Pharaoh tells Israel to take their flocks and herds too. He then asks an unusual request. He asks Moses to please bless Pharaoh! Verses 43-49 give us the regulations of the Passover.

Must Have Accepted Jesus Christ As Your Lord + Savior.

1. No stranger was to eat of it.
2. Any servant could eat of the meal after circumcision.
3. A foreigner and a hired hand cannot eat of the meal.
4. Has to be eaten at one house.
5. No meat can be taken out of the house.
6. Do not break any bones. — *Must be Perfect.*
7. The whole community of Israel must keep it.
8. All males living in house must be circumcised, including strangers.
9. No uncircumcised male may eat it.
10. The same law applies to the citizen, as well as the stranger living among them.

Notes: Why did God send the Plagues on Egypt?
1. They gave a great visual manifestation of the mighty power of the Lord (Exodus 9:16).
2. They were a heavenly visitation of God, a lesson to Pharaoh and the Egyptians for their ill treatment of the Hebrews (Exodus 10:6).
3. They were a judgment from God upon the sin of Egypt (Num. 33:4).

4. They were a sign that Jehovah was far above all other gods (Exodus 18:10).

5. They were a solemn promise to other nations that God would curse those who cursed the Israelites (Gen. 12:3, Josh. 2:8-9, I Sam. 4:8).

The Prophetic Forecast of the Plagues (God's future judgment upon the world).

1. God will send two witnesses to work miracles before their enemies (Revelation 11:3-6).

2. Their enemies will also perform miracles (Rev. 13:7).

3. God will hide His own people from them (Rev. 7:4; 12:6).

4. 1/3 of the seas will again turn into blood (Rev. 8:8; 16:4-5).

5. Satanic frogs will appear (Rev. 16:13).

6. A plague of locusts will be sent (Rev. 9:2-11).

7. God will send boils (Rev. 16:2).

8. Terrible hail and fire shall fall (Rev. 8:7).

9. There shall be awful darkness (Rev. 16:10).

10. Just as Pharaoh did not repent of his work, so will the evil men in the time to come (Rev. 9:20-21).

11. Demons will be loosed on the multitudes (Rev. 9:15).

Taken from: *Gleanings in Exodus* by A.W. Pink (pages 58-63)

Devotional Reading: Exodus 7-12

Memory Verses: Romans 9:14-18, Psalms 105:1-5, 106:1-5, 103:1-4; 8-10.

LESSON 4

MAN VERSUS GOD

Exodus 13:1-15:21

The Presentation of the Firstborn (13:1-16)

As the children of Israel moved out into their freedom, they were to dedicate their firstborn sons to the Lord God Almighty. In verse three, the Israelites were to commemorate this day as the day of deliverance. Israel was now free to enter the land flowing with "milk and honey." This dedication of the firstborn was a representation of the whole family. This would be an ordinance that Israel would keep from year to year according to verse 10.

The Provision of God (13:17-22)

The Lord led Israel through Goshen to the brink of the Red Sea. In verse 17, we find that an easier route, but certainly dangerous route, could have been through the land of the Philistines. God sometimes does not lead us in the easy ways, because He knows that the easy way can in the end be the most destructive way. This is true, because sometimes the easy way can actually rob us of strength that we can only get when times are hard. The easy way is not always the best way. Satan loves it when God's people take the easy way. He knows that when a Christian takes the easy way out, it will rob the Christian of spiritual growth and power in the end. In verse 21, we find that God led the people in the day by a cloud, and He led the people in the night by a pillar of fire.

The Parting of the Red Sea (14)

In this chapter, we see one of the most devastating military defeats in human history. We see the beginning

of the downfall of Egypt. After this time, history shows us that Egypt never again rose to world power. She would now begin to fade as a world power. In verse 4, God allowed Pharaoh to gather his forces and follow Israel to the Red Sea with the intent of destroying the Hebrews. God would allow this to show His power over the affairs of men. In verses 11-12, we see the faith of men in play. The people began to blame Moses when they knew that Pharaoh was coming to destroy them. They said, "Was it because there were no graves in Egypt that you brought us to the wilderness to die? Didn't we say to you in Egypt, 'leave us alone; let us serve the Egyptians'? It would have been better for us to serve the Egyptians than to die in the wilderness." Moses responds in verse 13-14. Moses tells them not to be afraid. He instructs all of Israel to stand still and see the salvation that the Lord would bring that day. Moses told them that the Egyptians that they saw that day would be gone forever. Moses reminds them that the Lord will fight for them. All Israel needed to do was to be peaceful. At this point God tells Moses to hold out Aaron's rod over the Red Sea. When this was done in verse 21, God sent a strong east wind and divided the water into two giant walls of water! God had commanded his creation to stand in allegiance to the faith of his people. The ground was dry, with not one ounce of moisture. Pharaoh pursued at his demise. After the people were on the other side, God returned the sea to its natural borders. This deluge destroyed Pharaoh's army.

The Praise of Moses and the People (15:1-21)

In verses 2-3, we see some interesting characteristics about God. We see that God is our source of strength and encouragement. He is our helper and our salvation. God is all-powerful. He is all-seeing. God is all-knowing. God is holy. He is our guide and provider. The next stanza in this song explains what God did to Pharaoh. God parted the Red Sea with the wind of His nostrils, and the army sank and drowned. The third stanza reminds us that there is none like God. Jehovah is greater than all.

Word Study:

A. Yeast (13:3)—Used to make bread rise and fill out.

B. Unleavened (15:7)—Bread without yeast.

C. Ordinance (13:10)—A way of doing things.

D. Hemmed (14:3)—tied into and unable to move.

E. Exalted (15:1)—Honored and respected.

F. Majestic (15:6)—Wonderful

G. Surging (15:8)—Moving ahead with power.

Devotional Reading: Exodus 13-15

Memory Verses: Exodus 15:1-2:11 Psalm 18:1-2

Notes to Remember: Moses and the people of Israel were in the desert. What was Moses going to do with them? They had to be fed, and feeding 2.3 million people requires a lot of food. According to the Quartermaster General of the army, it is reported that Moses would have to have 1,500 tons of food each day. To bring that much food each day, two freight trains each a mile long would be required! They were out in the desert, and they would have to have firewood to use in cooking the food. This would take 4,000 tons of wood and a few more freight trains, each a mile long, just for one day. And just think, they were forty years in transit. Oh, yes, they would have to have water. If they only had enough to drink and wash a few dishes, it would take 11 million gallons each day, and a freight train with tank cars 1,800 miles long, just to bring water! They also had to get across the Red Sea in one night. If they went on a narrow path, double file, the line would be 800 miles long and would require 30 days and nights to get through. There had to be a space in the Red Sea, 3 miles wide, so that they could walk 5,000 abreast to get over in one night. There was another problem. Each time they camped at the end of the day, a campground two-thirds the size of Rhode Island was required, or a total of 750 square miles. Think of it! This much space just for nightly camping. Do you think Moses figured all this out before he left Egypt? You see, Moses believed God. God took care of these things for him! Now, do you think God has any problem taking care of all your needs?

LESSON 5

DELIVERANCE

Exodus 15:20-18:27

The Pouting of the People (Exodus 15:20-17:7)

With freedom comes responsibility. As the people of Israel set out on their new found freedom, they come to a water hole by the name of Marah. Marah is a Hebrew word for bitter. The water was bitter and possibly not fit for drinking. It may even have been poisonous. In verse 25, Moses cuts down a tree and casts it into the water hole, thus making it sweet or fit to drink. In verse 27, the people of Israel come to the water hole of Elim. Here was the place of the "palms." Here, God gave the people rest and good water to drink. In these verses, the people pouted about the water that was given to them. In chapter 16 and verses 1-36, we see that the people began to pout about their food. This comes after they have now entered the plains of Zin, or the plains of the Arabian peninsula. In verse 3, the people accused Moses of bringing them out into the wilderness to starve them. In verse 4, God gave the people a small wafer-like honey-filled item called "manna." God gave Israel guidelines, however. They were to gather only enough for their family for one day and no more. On the sixth day, they could gather double the amount. Another form of nourishment that God gave

129

was meat. This meat came from a small bird called a quail. Israel could eat manna in the morning and quail at night. Those who thought that they had gathered too much found it to be just the right amount. According to verse 23, if Israel tried to keep food for the next day, it would turn to worms! They could not gather on the Sabbath. It was God's day, and God was to be set aside and worshiped. We see this in verse 23.

Some, however, tried to gather on the Sabbath, but to no avail. It would rot as soon as they picked it up. In verse 31, manna is described as a white coriander seed that tasted like honey. Israel, in order to show reverence and worship to God, took a basket of manna and placed it in the Ark of the Covenant as a symbol of God's provision for His people Israel. Israel ate this manna for forty years. Numbers 11:7-9 and Psalms 78:24-25 describe what manna looked like.

Next, the people pouted about their lack of water. In chapter 17:1-7, we find the camp of Israel camped next to Rephidim. Here, water was scarce and the people accused Moses once again of not caring. They accused Moses of bringing them out to thirst to death. At this point, the people were ready to stone Moses to death. In verse 6, God instructed Moses to strike the rock, and water would come forth.

The Protection from Above (Exodus 17:8-16)

We see a new leader emerge in this chapter. This young man named Joshua, which is Hebrew for Jesus, would later become a significant figure and leader in the life of Israel. He had come along with another man named Caleb. Joshua would become the military commander of Israel. In verse 8-10, Israel is face to face with the blood-thirsty and wicked pagan Amalekites. Joshua and Israel confronted the Amalekites in battle. Up on a nearby hill was Moses. As long as Moses held up his hands, the Israelites won. When

Moses' hands grew tired, they took rock and put it under him, and Moses sat on it. Aaron and Hur held Moses' hands up so that Israel would overcome the Amalekite army with the sword. According to verse 14, Moses wrote all this in a book. After the victory, Moses erected an altar. The altar was called Jehovah-Nissi. This is the Hebrew name which means, "God is our banner!"

The Principles of Leadership (18:1-27)

Chapter eighteen of Exodus is an exciting chapter, for it provides leadership lessons from the life of Moses. In verse one, Moses' father-in-law named Jethro comes to Moses because Jethro sees that Moses is burdened down with judging the nation of Israel. Verse fourteen shows us that Moses was judging and hearing cases from sun-up to sun-down. Here, Jethro introduced the principle of delegation. Moses' reply was that the people came to him to ask of God. Moses decided between them and taught them of God's statutes and laws. In verses 17-18, Jethro reminds Moses that this is not good. He told Moses that he would only wear himself out. Jethro told Moses that he could not do it alone. Verses 21-22 gives the plan for delegation. Moses was to select able men from all of the people. These men were to fear God. They were to be truthful men who hated dishonest gain. Moses was to place them as rulers over thousands, hundreds, fifties, and tens. They were known as judges. From then on, every great case was to come to Moses. The small cases were to be judged by these judges themselves. This would lighten the load for Moses.

Basic Truths to Remember

Manna was a type of Christ

As manna was sent from heaven above, so was Christ. Jesus several times referred to himself as the bread of life. Manna had to be gathered early in the morning. The psalmist said "Oh, satisfy us early...." It was their only true food of power. Christ is our only source of strength and power. Manna was sweet as honey. The Bible tells us to "taste and see that the Lord is good!"

The Rock was a type of Christ

"Just as the life-giving water flowed from the rock, so does eternal life flow from the Rock, Christ Jesus. And as the water was there for all to take it, so is salvation available for all who lay hold of it by faith (John 1:12). As thirst is quenched by water, so spiritual thirst is satisfied forever by faith in Christ" (John 4:14) Harper Study Bible.

Jethro a type of Christ

Christ forces us to realize that He alone holds the key to power and guidance in our lives. The key to having right priorities is obedience to Jesus and His Holy Word. Jethro calls Moses to face his major tasks and get his priorities right: 1. Moses' first task was to be an intercessor, to represent the people before God. 2 Moses' next task was to be a teacher to Israel, teaching them the words of God. 3. Moses' last task was to be an administrator, selecting capable men who could help rule the people. We see this in verses 19-21.

The Four characteristics for the men who would share "judicial" responsibility with Moses

1. They were to be "able" men.
2. They were to "fear" God.
3. They were to be "truthful" men.
4. They were to "hate" dishonest gain.

Word Study:

1. Omer (16:16)— A bushel of.

2. Maggots (16:20)—Fly larvae.

3. Coriander Seed (16:31)—A small heart-shaped chip-like nut.

4. Ephah (16:36)— A basket of.

5. Scroll (17:14)— Parchment fabric from flax or reeds.

6. Arrogantly (17:11)—To act above or over without consideration

7. Dispute (17:16)— To argue

Devotional Reading: Exodus 16-18

Memory Verses: Psalm 103:1-4

LESSON 6

INSTRUCTIONS

Exodus 19

The Covenant Made (Exodus 19)

In chapter 19 and verse 2, the Israelites encamped at the foot of Mount Sinai. Here, God would appear to His people in a thick cloud. The people at this time had to sanctify or set themselves apart unto God. They were to have their clothes washed. In verse 12, the Israelites were not to touch the border nor go up onto the mount. If they broke this boundary, they would surely die! Only Moses and Aaron were permitted to go up the mountain.

Introduction to the Law

The first four standards were "heavenly," and had to do with Israel's relationship with God. The final six standards were "earthly," and had to do with Israel's relationship with others. These standards would be called the "10 Commandments." This word comes from the Greek word "Deka Logous" or "Decalogue." These were also called "The Testimony," or the testimony of God's will. They were also called "The Covenant," or the agreed responsibilities of the people. There are three parts or divisions to this law. The laws of God were more than just the ten that

God gave Moses at this time. In Exodus 20:1-26, God gave Israel the "Moral Law." This governed the private life of the people. In Exodus 21:1-24:11, God gave Israel the "Ceremonial Laws." These laws governed the public life of the people. The last set of laws were called the "Monarchical Laws." In Exodus 24:12-32:18, these laws would govern the religious life of the Israelites. God gave the law to enable man to enhance his relationship with God and others. It protected the people from stealing from one another and harming each other. The law would enable Israel to live in harmony together.

Devotional Reading: Exodus 19,20

Memory Verses: Exodus 20:1-20, Psalm 18:1

STORY 1/21

LESSON 7

FREEDOM'S SONG

Exodus 20

Discussion:

As stated earlier, the first four commandments were directed to man's relation with God. Israel was not to have any other gods. They were not to worship made up gods, or as the Bible puts it, "graven images." Israel was not to take God's name in vain, or with disrespect. They were to keep the Sabbath day for being with God.

The last six commandments were directed to man's relation with his fellow man. The Israelites were to honor their parents. They were not to kill each other. They were not to commit adultery with each other. They were not to

139

steal from each other. They were not to bear false witness against each other. Lastly, they were not to be jealous of each other's good fortunes. In commandment one, God

let the people of Israel know that He was not just speaking of wooden idols. God wanted them to know that anything that took their attention from Him could be categorized as a god. We are to give God our sole undivided life. God demands our total life, attention, and commit-

ment. Idolatry occurs when we place anything before, or over God as the first place of our affection and obedience. So in a capsule, command number one deals with our priority towards God. God expects total commitment.

Commandment two has to do with other idols or images. This commandment does not forbid trophies or statues. It does forbid worshipping and showing allegiance to trophies or statues. Here is a solemn warning from God. God is a jealous God. God will punish those who bow down to idols. Nothing must be allowed to be above God's place in our life. God, according to this commandment, demands total loyalty.

Commandment three deals with not abusing God's name. There are several ways that we can use God's name in the wrong way. According to Leviticus 18:21, one can use God's name in profanity. Romans 10:9-10 teaches that when we do not call on the Lord for salvation, we profane His name. We can also profane the name of the Lord when we pray for salvation but do not mean it. Another way, according to Numbers 30:2, is the breaking of vows. God expects us to keep our promises. So one must remember that when we pray in "Jesus" name, what we are praying is in agreement with the will of God. This statement alone lets us know that when we pray, we must be sincere as to what we pray for. On the other hand, Matthew 10:32 teaches us that when we confess Jesus before other men, we glorify God. Joel 2:32 states that when we call for salvation, this magnifies God. John 4:24 teaches us to speak the name of God in worship. We are to lift up His holy name. So in conclusion, God's name must only be used out of praise and reverence. To profane God's name means to speak or joke irreverently of holy things. Hypocrisy means to have showy, empty displays of humility and religious activity. Empty vows means to make a promise to the Lord and then brake it. So in this commandment, God is demanding total sincerity and total reverence.

Commandment four speaks of remembering the Sabbath day, and that we are to keep it holy. The purpose of the Sabbath is two-fold. According to Genesis 2:3, the Sabbath was set-aside by God for the purpose of resting. In John 4:24, the Lord reminded us that the Sabbath was set aside to worship God. The Sabbath was originally on Saturday, from six in the morning to six at night. During these hours, Israel was not to work. Israel was to spend time with family and with Jehovah. When Jesus Christ arose, things changed. We now worship and rest on the first day of the week called Sunday. A day that is hallowed is one which is set aside for God's special purposes. Jesus said in Mark 2:27, "The Sabbath was made for man, not man for the Sabbath." This day is kept when it glorifies and focuses on God. "True worship acknowledges the 'true worth-ship' of God." Commandment four tells us that we are to be totally devoted to God. God has set aside a day for renewal and direction.

Commandment five starts the relationship of man to man. It comes after four commands that deal with our relationship with God. The reason is that our relation with God is closely linked with our relation to our fellow man, and visa versa. So it is natural that the last six deal with our fellowship with our fellow man! In Exodus 20:12, God tells us to "Honor our parents." Why does God use the parents first? The reason is that we learn to "get along" with society in the home. According to Exodus 21:15-17, a child is not to retaliate or curse his parents. Ephesians 6:1 tells the child to obey his parents as unto the Lord. The same passage adds long life as a blessing in the obeying of the parents as well. The Bible also teaches parents that we are to provide for our children. We are to be an example. Parents are to lead their children to Christ. The blessing of all this is a happy, fulfilled, long, prosperous life! The question comes though, "When is it alright to disobey?" The answer is simple, but tough. When what we are asked to do is in direct opposition of what the Bible teaches, then we must graciously disobey. The Bible teaches that the wrong kind of disobedience leads to witchcraft and rebellion. The definition of discipline is training to live according to boundaries and rules and instruction and exercise designed to bring about proper conduct and action. True discipline brings about a state of order and obedience by training.

The family is so important in the social development of a child. Why is this so? God made the family the primary unit of society. You have probably heard this before, "As the family goes, so goes the nation." The family unit is God's breeding ground for social preparation in society. We can honor our parents by obeying in our younger years, listening in our older years, and nurturing through all their years. To honor means to respect, listen, ask questions, and reverence as a sacred trust. To dishonor means to show hatred and disbelief, to question with doubt. This leads to wrong choices, short lives, and an unfulfilled life. The family is God's primary and first unit of society. The family is used by God to teach us how to relate to our fellow man around us. The fifth commandment teaches total unity.

Commandment six teaches us not to murder. According to Exodus 20:13, we are not to kill another human being. This does not forbid the killing of animals and plants (Gen. 9:3). Exodus 22:2 deals with the killing of another, while trying to defend ourselves. If the other dies, God does not hold the one being attacked guilty. Titus 3:1 tells us that we must kill in times of war and protection of others.Genesis 9:6 gives the government the right to put to death those who deserve such. This commandment refers to the act of violence that arises out of feelings of greed, jealousy, bitterness, and malice. Life is always considered to be God's gift. Life is precious and sacred. No man has the right to destroy what God has given. The biblical sense of murder means to end the life of another on purpose. Murder means to end the influence and contribution of another life. Murder steals the gift that God has given to another human being. An example of this was Adam and Eve when they sinned (Gen. 3:7-10), Cain and Abel (Gen. 4:8), John the Baptist (Mark 6:14-29), and Jesus (Luke 23). Murder is against the very image of God. One who maliciously and premeditatedly murders shall be put to death! This commandment deals with personal responsibility.

Commandment seven deals with fidelity. Exodus 20:14 tells us not to "commit adultery." God has set apart sex for the purpose of two things: procreation and pleasure between a husband and a wife (Genesis 1:28, 9:1). Marriage is based on trust and commitment to God and the one to whom you are married. The Bible teaches us that there are four actions that lead to adultery.They all begin with "L's":

looking, lusting, lying to self and others, and living it out. Adultery causes divorce. The Bible gives only two biblical grounds for divorce: adultery, and when a non-believer leaves a believer for another relationship. However, God's people are expected to live to a higher standard: "one man for one woman for a life-time." To see how serious Israel took this command, read II Samuel 11 & 12, Job 24:13, Isaiah 1:21, and Hosea 1:2. This commandment deals with marital honesty and trustworthiness.

Commandment eight deals with honesty and financial integrity. In Exodus 20:15, we find that God says that we are not to steal from others, especially from Him. It implies taking something that does not belong to us, or taking something that belongs to another person. Some examples of this would be : vandalizing, or taking things from others without their permission; kidnapping someone against their will; taking away someone's purity; slandering someone's reputation; being dishonest in business; being dishonest in our lives with others; not tithing, or giving to God what is rightfully His. When we settle ownership in our lives, giving is not a question. Theft is an invasion of privacy and a denial of self-responsibility. Ephesians 4:28 tells us how to conquer stealing. It tells us to work with our own hands, and don't steal anymore. Stealing is taking what does not rightfully belong to me. In order for one to take something, they must have the right of ownership. To have the right of ownership, one must have paid for the thing they take. There must be proof of ownership. There must be a receipt. It must be a gift given. The full price must have been given or paid. Ownership is violated when privacy, property, possession, personhood, character, reputation, integrity, and anothers ownership is taken away. Commandment eight has to do with just plain old honesty of character.

Commandment nine deals with integrity and personal truthfulness. Exodus 20:16 says not to lie! John 8:44 tells us that the devil is a liar, and the father of all lies and liars. John 14:6 tells that the Father and the Son are the true source of all truth. The basic truth of the matter is that God's children cannot lie and get away with it (Acts 5:1-11). Lying may bring us short-term gains, but it always results in long-term losses. The best way to avoid lying is to do nothing that needs to be hid. Warning: "All liars shall have their part in the lake of fire" (Rev. 21:8). Telling lies causes mistrust, hurt, and more lies. The words that you say should be truthful and accurate. This spirit is manifested in several ways. It is manifested in how we treat people; by how we deal with others; exaggerating and overstating things; by giving false information, or not stating the truth; by tale-bearing and gossiping; by misleading people; by forging and fraud; by lying to authorities. This commandment has to do with personal honesty.

Commandment ten deals with security. God told Israel not to be jealous of another's possessions. We see this in Exodus 20:17. To "covet" means to want that which belongs to someone else. A person who is covetous has a desire and longing to have not just his many possessions, but the possessions of others. His motto is: "What is mine is mine, and what's yours is mine too!" To desire what someone else has is to be dissatisfied with what God has richly blessed you with. Warning: Do not be willing to give or sell your life/soul for worldly temporal wealth (Mark 10:24,25). Covetousness is a desire for another's position, possession, posterity, and pleasure. This command differs from all the others in that it deals with the direction of the heart. It deals with our faith and what it is dependent upon. There are two things about a covetous man. He will never be satisfied, and he will lean on material things before God. We must remember that money in itself is not evil. It is the "LOVE" of money that is the root of all evil.

Memory Verses: Psalm 18:2

LESSON 8

FREEDOM'S INGRATITUDE

Exodus 21:1-24:18

Discussion:

The Lord God Jehovah kept Moses up on top of Mount Sinai for forty days. God was giving Moses more than just ten commandments. God gave Moses some 209 other laws. Those laws

were broken up into three basic divisions: there were the social laws, the religious laws, and the ceremonial laws. We shall look at just two of them in depth. First, we shall look at the social laws. There were four basic laws socially for Israel. We see these recorded in Exodus 21:1-22:17. There were laws concerning servants (21:1-11). There were laws dealing with murder and manslaughter (21:12-17). There were laws pertaining to kidnapping and child discipline (21:18-36). Then there were laws about theft, vandalism, and fornication (22:1-17).

The next set of laws were the religious laws. There were seven of these laws. There were laws dealing with witchcraft

149

(22:18). There were laws about having immoral relations with animals (22:19). There were laws against sacrificing to idols (22:20). There were also laws concerning the oppressed (22:21-23). There were laws about slandering people and bearing false witness against others (23:1-9). There were laws concerning the Sabbath day (23:10-12). The last set of laws dealt with the three "Holy Feasts" (23:14-19). This set of laws was three-fold. There was the law of the "Unleavened Bread" (12:15), the "Seven Offerings" or the "Atonement" (Lev. 23:15-21), and lastly, there was the "Feast of Tabernacles" or "Holy Convocation" (Lev. 23:33-36).

In chapter 23:20-24:18, God gives the children of Israel an angel. This angel *Jesus Christ* would keep them along the way. The angel would bring them to the place that Jehovah had prepared for them. In verse 21, the people were to pay attention, to be obedient to him. Israel was not to strive against him. In verse 22, God said that He would be an enemy to Israel's enemies, and that He would be against those who were against Israel. God reminded Israel that they were not to bow down to other gods. They were not to serve these gods. Israel was not to do the works of these gods. In chapter 24, Moses erects an altar with 12 stones that would represent the nation of Israel as a memorial to the gracious leading of God from Egypt to Mount Sinai. After this altar is erected, Moses then reads the Book of the Covenant to all of Israel. In verse twelve, God gives Moses the "Tables of Stones." The law and the commandments were written for Israel's learning. In verse 14, Moses puts

Aaron and Hur in charge of teaching the people the law and commandments. God would make His presence visible to Israel. During the night, God would lead Israel by a "Pillar of Fire." During the day, God would lead Israel by an "Overshadowing Cloud." Verse 18 tells us that Moses was with God on the mountain for forty days and nights.

Word Study:

    A. Demolish (23:24)—To utterly tear down.

    B. Encounter (23:27)—To come face to face with.

    C. Hornet (23:28)—A small green bee

    D. Snare (23:33)—To lay trap, to trap or cripple someone or thing.

    E. Sapphire (24:10)—A blue jewel.

    F. Consuming (24:18)—To burn up or take in.

Project: Read Exodus 23:30-33 and list the four "Do Nots," and list the "I Wills."

Devotional Reading: Exodus 23:30-33; 24:1-18

Memory Verses: Psalm 100:4

WHAT DOES GOD WANT FROM HIS PEOPLE

Introduction to the Tabernacle

Discussion:

There are five different names given in regard to the Tabernacle. In Exodus 26:36, It is called the "Tent." In Exodus 25:9, it is called the "Tabernacle." In Exodus 25:8, it is called the "Sanctuary." In Exodus 29:42-44, it is called the "Temple of the Congregation." In Numbers 1:50, it is called the "Temple of the Testimony." There are three meanings of the Tabernacle. The tabernacle is a type, a visible illustration of that heavenly tabernacle in which God has His throne. The tabernacle is a type of Jesus Christ, who is the meeting place between man and God. The tabernacle is a type of peace in the relationship of the communion of Christ with all His children. The tabernacle was a holy place. It was plain and earthly in outward appearance. It was God's dwelling place. It was the place where God met with man. It was the middle of Israel's camp. It was the place where the blood was preserved. It was the place where intercession was made. It was the place where the priestly family was fed. It was the place of forgiveness. Lastly, it was approached through the tribe of Levi.

The Outline of the rest of Exodus is as follows:

The Tabernacle Designed--(Chapters 25-31).

The Tabernacle Delayed--(Chapter 32-34).

The Tabernacle Completed--(Chapters 35-40).

Project: Draw the design of the Tabernacle: Page 137 in work book

Devotional Reading: Hebrews 9:1-28

Memory Verse: Exodus 20:1-10

RELATIONSHIPS TAKE THREE PEOPLE

Exodus 25-31

Discussion:

God now instructs Moses to make manifest on Earth what God had already had plans for in Heaven. God would use the people to build the church as He does today. They were to give of themselves by faith, trusting God to supply the resources. In chapter 25:1-9, Moses collects the offering from God's people to build the Tabernacle. These offerings were to come from the people who were willing to give. This offering would come from three different areas, as the people were able to give. The first area was different metals that were needed for the rings and nails. The people gave "gold." This gold would represent beauty, purity, worth, and lasting quality. They gave "silver." Silver would represent the ransom or atonement needed for salvation and forgiveness. They gave "brass." Brass would come to represent God's place of judgement. Then they gave "precious stones" or "diamonds." The stones would come to represent strength!

Another area of resources came from fabrics. The people gave four different kinds of fabric. They gave "fine linen." This fabric would represent God's righteousness.

They gave "goat's hair." This fabric represented a servant's heart. The next fabric was that of "rams skin." This would represent devotion. The last fabric was " badger skin." Badger skin would come to be a symbol of God's holiness.

The last area would come from the color area. The people of Israel gave many different colors. White represented God's purity and righteousness. Red would be a symbol of God's salvation, sacrifice, and redemption. Scarlet/Black would be a symbol of judgement, sin, and death. Purple would be a symbol of royalty and kingship. Lastly, blue would come to known for heaven, truth, and beauty.

The furniture is discussed in Exodus 25:10-30:38.

Word Study:
   A. Fragrant (25:6)—A smell well pleasing to the nose.
   B. Acacia Wood (25:10)—A water-repellent wood.
   C. Cubit (25:10)—18 inches or from the elbow to the middle finger.
   D. Ladles (25:29)—Bowl-shaped spoons.
   E. Grating (27:4)—Rubbing against a fence or an Iron fence.
   F. Molding (30:3)—Trimming

Devotional Reading: Ex. 25:10-40; 27:1-18; 30:1-10, 17-21

Memory Verse: Exodus 20:11-20

LESSON 11

THE LAW OF DIRECTION

Exodus 25-31

The Tabernacle (26:1-37)

Verses 1-14 of Exodus 26 describe how the curtains would be made and the material used. There were to be ten curtains. They were to be made of fine woven linen, blue, purple, and scarlet yarn, with cherubim designs worked into them. They were to be coupled together. The loops on the curtains were to be made of blue yarn. The clasps for the curtains were to be made of gold. The curtain that would go over the tabernacle was to be made from goat's hair. Israel was to make eleven of these curtains. Over the tent was added red dyed ram's skins. Over this was laid the badger's skins. In verses 15-25, frames were to be made for the southern and northern ends of the tabernacle. There were to be twenty for each end. The bases for these frames were to be made out of silver. There were to be six on the west end and eight on the east end. In verses 26-29, the crossbars that held the frames together were to be made out of acacia wood. The center bars were to extend from end to end. They were to be made out of gold.

The Tabernacle is described for us in verses 30-35. Behind the curtain that would separate the Holy Place from the Holy of Holies was to be placed the Ark of the Covenant. In the holy place, the Seven Golden

Candlesticks, the Table of Shewbread, and the Altar of Incense were strategically placed. The entrance curtain to the Tabernacle was made of blue, purple, scarlet linen. Five sockets of brass were to hold the curtain down in place together. Exodus 27:9-19 describes for us the courtyard. In chapter 30: 11-16, we have described the "atonement money." Each Jew, whether poor or rich had to give a shekel when they were counted. This giving was called a "ransom." This giving

would support the priest in their work of service in the tabernacle.

The "anointing oil" was made of spices. According to chapter 30:23-24, 500 shekels of liquid myrrh, 250 shekels of fragrant cinnamon, 250 shekels of fragrant calamus, 500 shekels of cassia, and a "pinch" of olive oil were used as the anointing oil. This oil would be used to anoint the tabernacle and all of the vessels used in the tabernacle. This would be a symbol of sanctification unto "the holiness of God." The individuals who were anointed were Aaron and his sons. They were to be "separated" unto the Lord to serve the Lord God Almighty!

Israel was not to use this oil to anoint other men, and they were not to make any other oils with this oil. According to verse 33, if they disobeyed God on this, they would be cut off from God!

Word Study:
  A. Sea Cows (26:14)—Badgers
  B. Census (30:12)—Count of the people for tax purposes.
  C. Shekel (30:13)—.20cents
  D. Gerahs (30:13)—.01 cent
  E. Consecrate (30:29)—To surrender and dedicate unto God alone.

Devotional Reading: Ex. 36:1-37; 27:9-19; 30:11-16; 22-33

Memory Verse: Matthew 22:37-40

LESSON 12

PLANS FOR GOD'S HOUSE

Exodus 25-31

The Priest (28:1-29:46) *Now Jesus Christ*

To be a priest, one had to be a Levite. The priest was the mediator or "go between," between God and man. In the patriarchal age, the father of the families acted as the priest. Some examples are Noah (in Genesis 8:20), Abraham (Genesis 12:7), Jacob (Genesis 35:7), and Job (Job 1:5). The two great priests of the Old Testament were Melchizadek and Aaron. Melchizadek was a priest-king. His genealogy is not given, thus we do not know his beginning or ending. He was a priest of the Most High God. He was a definite type of Christ (Heb. 6:20-7:3). Aaron was the first priest appointed by God. Aaron's sons were appointed priests with him. Aaron was at the foundation of all the priesthood. Aaron made the atonement for the sins of the people, by sprinkling blood upon the Mercy Seat. He represented the people in the presence of God.

The Priestly Garments (28:1-43)

Why did Israel have to make sacred garments for Aaron? God wanted to set the High Priest apart from the regular priests. The High Priest would come to be a symbol

161

of the Lord Jesus Christ and His ministry. The regular priests would come to represent the believer. These garments would be made for the beauty and glory of God and His holiness. The garments were to be made of a breastplate, an ephod, a robe, an embroidered coat, a mitre, and a girdle. The ephod was made out of gold, blue and purple, with scarlet fine-twined linen. The ephod contained two onyx stones that were engraved with the names of the children of Israel. The names were arranged in the birth order of the brothers. Six names were on one stone. The stones were to be fitted into a hollow filigree setting. The stones were then placed on each shoulder. Aaron was to display these stones on his shoulders as a memorial that God would always carry His people. The breastplate is described in chapter 28:15-30. The breastplate was to be made of gold, blue, purple, and fine-twined scarlet linen as the ephod. The breastplate was made as a square. There were to be four rows of the stones. All were different stones. The first row consisted of Sardius, Topaz, and Carbuncle. The second row consisted of Emerald, Sapphire, and Diamond. The third row consisted of Liguire, Agate, and Amethyst. The last row consisted of Beryl, Onyx, and Jasper. There were twelve stones that represented the twelve tribes of Israel. The breastplate was to be tied to the Ephod.

The breastplate also bore upon itself the "Urim and Thummim." These names mean "the lights and the perfections." These items were probably intended to describe the nature of God, whose will the priests were to do and reveal. The Urim and the Thummim were kept in a pouch inside the breastplate. They were used to determine the will and direction of God.

The robe is described in verses 31-35. It was blue in color. Aaron had to wear the robe when he went into the Holy of Holies. At the bottom of the robe were bells that rang to let the people know that God had accepted Aaron. If the bells ever stopped ringing, it was a good sign that God had killed Aaron for sin. He had to be blameless from sin to enter into the Holy of Holies. The bells were golden. They were at the bottom of the robe. They demonstrated that God had accepted Aaron's offering.

The turban or head piece had a golden plate on the front that had engraved on it, "Holiness To The Lord." This golden piece was attached on the front of the turban with blue lace. This head piece was a symbol that the High Priest would bear the sin of the people. He had to bear all of the iniquity of the people to atone for all the people's sin. This would be a symbol of what Jesus would have to do for the sin of the whole world.

The tunic and sashes are seen in verses 39-41 of chapter 28. They were also made for the regular priests as well. They were beautiful, representing that all truth is beautiful. This was done to set apart the priest for the service of God.

The under garments were made to cover the nakedness. They went from the neck down to the knees. The priests were to wear these garments when ministering in the Holy Place. They had to wear them as a symbol that when we, as saints, work for God, we must keep our lives pure in order to be effective in our service for God.

In chapter 29:1-46, we see the consecration of the priests. In the consecration service, a bull and two rams

without blemish had to be used. Unleavened bread was also used. It had to be mixed with oil, along with wheat. At the entrance of the tabernacle, the priest had to be washed with water, as well as oil poured over their heads. Offerings were then made. There were three offerings. The first was called the "Burnt Offering." This offering was intended to be a symbol of Jesus' sacrifice for the sin of the whole world. The second offering was called the "Wave Offering." This offering, which was wholly given, was symbolic of their total consecration to the Lord and God's judgments. The "Heave Offering" was for the priestly food. This was done by moving the portion of the animal toward the altar and then away from it, symbolizing that this was to be offered to God and then given back to the priest by God. The consecration or "ordination" of Aaron and his sons took seven days. According to verse 37, the priests made atonement and sanctified themselves to God. Three things were to be offered upon entering the "Tent of Meeting." A lamb, meat, and a drink offering were given. The Lord would meet them at the entrance. Verses 45-46 tells us why God did all of this. He wanted the people to know that He dwelt in their midst.

Word Study:
  A. Dignity (28:2)—Respect for self.
  B. Filigree (28:11)— Bowl-shaped sockets of gold.
  C. Pomegranates (28:33)—A seed that looks like a small green tomato.
  D. Aroma (29:18)—A Fragrance
  E. Ordination (29:27)—To appoint or approve.
  F. Ephah (29:40)—A bushel.
  G. Hin (29:40)—A pinch of something.

Project: Label the parts of the High Priest's Robe.

Devotional Reading: Exodus 28:1-29:46; 31:1-18

Memory Verse: Psalm 127:1

GOD'S HOUSE DESIGNED FOR REFUGE

Exodus 32-34

Discussion:

While Moses is up on Mount Sinai receiving the Law from God, the people get inpatient waiting on God. They ask Aaron to make them a god that they can see and worship. Aaron gave in under the "peer pressure" and told the people to bring him their gold. Aaron then takes the gold and makes a golden calf. In verse six, the people then begin to sacrifice to this god. God sees this revelry and tells Moses to descend down  the mountain, for the people were worshiping false gods. In verse 8, the people were giving credit to these gods for leading them out of Egypt. In verse nine, God calls the Israeli people "stiff-necked." God then tells Moses to leave Him so that his wrath might wax hot against them, and that He might consume them, and then make them a great nation. Moses however intercedes for the people of Israel. He reminded God that if God killed all of the Jews, then Egypt would say that Moses only led the people out to destroy them. At this point, God "repented" of what He was going to do. Moses then goes down the mountain. When Moses gets down to the

foot of the mountain, he sees all manner of sin and wickedness. His anger burned, and he cast the tables out of his hands. Moses then takes the golden calf and burns it. He then grinds it into a fine powder and makes the people drink it with their water. Before Moses does this, he asks this question: "Who is on the Lord's side?" In verse 27, Moses tells each man to strap a sword to his side and go back and forth through the camp from one end to the other, slaying every man his brother, companion, and neighbor. Moses then tells the people that he would go up before God and make an atonement for the people's sin. In verse 32, Moses asked God to please forgive their sins. Moses tells God that if He will not forgive Israel, then God must blot out Moses from the book that God had written. The Lord answers that those who have sinned against God would be blotted out of His book. God reminds Moses that when the time came for Him to visit them, it would be for their sin! God punished Israel with a plague, according to verse 35.

According to verse 3 of chapter 33, God was not going to go with Israel into the promised land because Israel was a "stiff-necked" people. When the people heard this, they mourned and would not decorate themselves. At this time, the Tabernacle was outside Israel's campsite. In verse nine, God comes and stands at the door way as a cloudy pillar with Moses. This causes the people to rise up and worship God as well. In verse 11, God tells Moses that from now on, He would speak face-to-face with Moses as a man speaks with his friend. We see also in this verse, the next leader in the making. His name would come to be known as Joshua.

In chapter 33:12-23, Moses prays to God and asks God who would go up to the promised land. As Israel traveled, the other nations would know that they were different because of God's overshadowing mercy and grace towards them. We see in verses 18-19, the Glory of God revealed to Moses. God wants to reveal Himself to man today also. God said that He would make all His goodness to pass before Moses. God would proclaim His name. God said that He would have mercy on those He wanted to have mercy on, and that He would have grace on those he wanted to have grace on. The only thing that Moses would not see would be God's face. Moses did get to see the "hind parts" of God, as God passed by Moses.

In chapter 34:1-35, God renews His covenant with Moses. God remakes the 10 Commandments. In verse 10, God makes a covenant with Moses and promises to do marvels never yet done. God warns the people of Israel not to make covenants with strange nations, because such alliances could come back to be a snare to Israel down the road. God tells the people how to handle future idols. He instructs Israel to tear down their altars. God tells them to break their sacred images and to cut down their grove poles,or place of adultery.

Israel was reminded by God that they were to worship Jehovah only, because He was a jealous God. In verse 18, Israel was to commemorate this day with the "Feast of Unleavened Bread." This was to be done for seven days. On the first day, a first born calf was to be sacrificed to God. Israel was then to rest on the seventh day and on harvest days. The other two feasts that Israel was to celebrate during this week was the Feast of First Fruits, and the Feast of the Harvest. Three times a year, all of the men were to appear before God. When Israel came to the House of the Lord, they were to bring their first fruits. Moses was with God for a total of 40 days and 40 nights. When Moses finally came down from being in God's presence, Moses' face was so bright that, according to verses 29-30, Moses had to put a veil over his face. His face was so bright that no one could look at it.

Question: Does our life so shine that men see God and are shaken by His presence?

Word Study:

A. Indulge (32:6)—To be involved too much.

B. Revelry (32:6)—Uncontrolled passion.

C. Stiff-necked (32:9)— Hard-headed and stubborn.

D. Relent (32:12)—To give up to.

E. Atonement (32:30)—To cover for.

F. Prostitute (34:15)—A Harlot or woman of evil reputation.

G. Radiant (34:29)—To shine brilliantly.

Devotional Reading: Exodus 32-34

Basic Truths:

1. An idol is anything that we put ahead of God.

2. Human impatience is assuming that God is not here.

3. We are in danger when we don't live by faith. It becomes all us and not God.

4. Israel gave credit to their hand-made god for their deliverance when they knew better.

5. God is a merciful and just God. He must punish sin. No other person can "cover" my sins, they must be punished. Jesus is the only one, who through His sacrificial death on the cross can "cover" my sins.

6. "Repent" does not mean that God made a mistake. It simply means that God changed the way that He would deal with Israel's sin.

Memory Verse: Exodus 25:10

LESSON 14

THE TENT THAT GOD LIVES IN

Exodus 35-40

Discussion:

Exodus chapter 35:1-3 deals with the Sabbath Instructions. Chapter 35:4-29 deals with instructions in gathering Building Materials. Chapter 35:30-36:7 deals with the Workmen's Instructions on building the tabernacle. Two men were to head up this building project. The first was a man by the name of Bezaleel. Bezaleel was from the tribe of Judah. The Bible says that Bezaleel was a man full of the spirit of God. He was filled with wisdom, understanding and the knowledge in all kinds of workmanship. Bezaleel was an artist in designs. The other leader was a man named Aholiab. Aholiab was from the tribe of Dan. This man had the ability to teach to do all kinds of weaving. Chapter 36:8-39:31 gives us the details of the building of the Tabernacle. After the tabernacle was finished, God instructed Moses to do and inspection of the building. According to verse 32-43, the building was done according to all the Lord had commanded. Moses then comes behind and inspects and then blesses the work.

Exodus chapter 40:1-33, gives us the erection details.

The first piece of furniture put into the tabernacle was the Ark of The Covenant. After everything is done, the place is anointed with oil. The priests were washed and anointed by Moses. Aarons' sons were given coats and anointed as well. After all this was done in verses 34-38, God Himself covers the tent with a great cloud and the Glory of God filled the tents. The people knew it was time to move when the cloud moved. According to verse 38, a pillar of fire covered the tabernacle at night.

Conclusion to the Book of Exodus:

"In the beginning of Exodus, Israel was enslaved in Egypt and did not know that God was either near or aware of them. In the end of the book, they are free, redeemed people, on their way to the land of promise, accompanied and guided by the Almighty God Himself. So it has ever been. Those who have been redeemed by God are guided and sustained through the wilderness as they travel to the new land of promise. God always leads those whom He has redeemed."

Taken from: Laymen's Bible Commentary (Vol.2, p140)

Devotional Reading: Exodus 35:-36:7; 39:32-40:38

Memory Verses: I Corinthians 10:31, Exodus 35:21

INTRODUCTION TO LEVITICUS

Author: Moses

Where Written: Mount Sinai, before the wilderness journey.

When: 1450 B.C.

God's Roll: God, the Lawgiver of the third book of law.

God's Command: "Be ye Holy, for I am Holy."

Key Verse: Leviticus 20:7

Key Message: How can a sinful man approach a holy God?

Key Words: "Access and Holiness"

Leviticus Outline:

I.   The Way to God (Sacrifice). Chs. 1-10

II. The Walk with God (Sanctified). Chs. 11-20

III. The Worship of God (Service). Chs. 21-27

INTRODUCTORY NOTES FOR LEVITICUS:

There are three major teachings in the book of Leviticus. The first is that of consecration. God requires the absolute obedience of His people. The next is praise and worship. Praise and worship is a gift to God as an expression of love and gratitude. The last teaching is that of atonement. Atonement means at-one-ment. Atonement is the removal of the guilt of sin and its meaning (1:1).

Leviticus is a constructive/symbolic book. God is

speaking to us through the tabernacle and its meaning. It is a priestly book. God expects each person to bring his own gift (1:2). The New Testament companion book is the book of Hebrews.

The book of Leviticus deals with the sacrificial blood. There are three fundamental principles of redemption illustrated in the blood sacrifices of the Old Testament. There is the principle of the "Scapegoat." The one who offers presses his hand heavily on the forehead of the animal, thus identifying himself with it. In like manner, the believer identifies himself with the death, burial and resurrection of Christ through personal faith, which is perfectly pictured in the ordinances of baptism (see Rom. 6:3-11). The principle of substitution is the innocent animal, which was reckoned sinful, and suffered and died instead of the sinner. The animal sacrifices marvelously foreshadowed the substitutionary death of Christ on the behalf of sinners. (see Rom. 5:8; II Cor. 5:21; I Pet. 2:24; 3:18). Lastly, there is the principle of the "propitiation." This offering of the blood was a tangible and visible evidence that a life had been offered up. It is the blood of Jesus that satisfies the holiness of God, and allows a sinful man to be reckoned righteous in His sight (see Rom. 3:25; Heb. 9:22).

Taken from The Criswell Study Bible p. 129

LESSON 1

THE WAY TO GOD

Leviticus 1:1-10:20

Discussion:

The sacrifices in the book of Leviticus fall into two divisions. There were the sacrifices used to "approach" God for the purpose of establishing fellowship. In chapter one, we see the "burnt" offering. In the second chapter of Leviticus, we see the "grain" offering. In chapter three, we have the "peace" offering. The second division of sacrifices were used to "approach" God for the purpose of restoring fellowship. There were two types of offerings in this division. There was the "sin" offering in chapter 4, and the "trespass" offering in chapter 5.

The five offerings above are explained in depth in chapters 1:1-7:27. The burnt offering represented the "death" of Christ for the world. The grain offering, or also known as the "meal" offering depicted the "surrender" of Christ in service. The peace offering depicted the "fellowship" of Christ in relationships. The sin offering was a type of the "atonement" of Christ for sinners. The trespass offering showed "forgiveness" by Christ from the wrath of God.

Burnt bulls and lambs were the type of the death of Christ for sin. Christ bore our sin on Himself. This was the most precious sacrifice in the ancient tent.

Meal/Grain became the symbol of total devotion. This offering represented Christ coming to serve, and not to be served. Christ is the Bread of Life.

The peace offering was an offering of fellowship. [WORSHIP] This offering showed Christ dying for man's sin to "bridge" the gap from man to God.

The trespass offering [disobedience] showed that Christ even took care of trespasses against God. The blood cleanses the conscience (see the enclosed charts on the offerings).

The sin offering shows us Christ on the cross in the sinner's place. God holds us accountable for our sin.

In chapters 7:28-10:20, the people were to take care of their priests. God instructs them to give a "heave" offering. This is where the right shoulder of the sacrifice is given to the priest (Lev. 7:28-34). The priests were then "ordained" or confirmed. This ordination was performed in five steps. The priests were washed, anointed with oil, touched by blood, sprinkled with both oil and blood, and they were fed. The ordination took seven days.

The ministry is given in chapter 9:1-24. Aaron's first assignment was to make an atonement for himself. When this happened, the glory of God appeared, and the fire from heaven came upon the altar and consumed [Accepted] the burnt offering. When the people saw this, it caused them to shout and fall on their faces before God. When the priests were serving and offering up the offerings of God, it was a very serious and dangerous thing. God had a specific way of doing worship. In verses 1-10 of chapter 10, we have recorded for us what happens when priests violate the law of God. The two sons of Aaron decide to violate God's laws for offerings. They decide to offer a "strange" offering, and in verse two, both men are consumed by the fire that comes off the altar. The priest's walk with God is disclosed in chapters 11-20 of the book of Leviticus.

Word Study:
   A. Atonement (1:4)—To cover over.
   B. Unintentionally (4:1)—Not meaning to do something.
   C. Ceremonially (4:12)—Formally
   D. Restitution (5:16)—To pay back in the place of.
   E. Contribution (7:32)—To support or give support to.
   F. Ordination (8:22)—To approve and set apart for.
   G. Sanctification—To grow away from the world and towards God's Holiness.

Devotional Reading: Leviticus 1-5; 7:28-9:24

Memory Verses: Leviticus 20:7

Project: Write a short essay on "The Priest," "The High Priest" and "Our Great High Priest."

LESSON 2

THE WORSHIP OF GOD

Leviticus 21-27

Discussion:

God instituted holy times (holi-days) in the calendar of the Israelis so that His people would set aside many days of the year to meditate on Him, and to think about what He had done for them. These holy times were celebrated with "feasts." There were seven of them in number. They were called the "Seven Feasts of the Lord." The first feast was known as "The Feast of the Passover." The Passover was celebrated every spring at our Easter. It was like the Fourth of July for the Jews. The Passover commemorated the freeing of Israel from Egypt (Lev. 23:4-5). This celebration lasted one day. The next feast was that of "Unleavened Bread." This feast lasted seven days (23:6-8). There was the feast of the "First Fruits" (23:9-14). Chapter 23:15-22 records the feast of "Jubilee." This feast was also called "Pentecost." It was celebrated fifty days after the feast of "First Fruits." It was fifty days after the resurrection of Christ that the Holy Spirit descended upon the disciples, and the church was born. In chapter 23:26-32, we see the feast of "Atonement." On this day, the sins of the nation were confessed. On this day, Jehovah's relationship to His people was established. This was the only day in the year when the High Priest was permitted to enter the Holy of Holies. This is the spiritual highlight of the Jewish calendar year. The feast of "Tabernacles" was celebrated in the fall of the year. It lasted for one week. These days reminded the Israelis of their dependence upon Jehovah.

Chapter 25:1-8 talks about the "Sabbatical Year." This was every seventh year. During this year, the Jewish people could keep the excess of what was left over in their surplus. The next great year was the year of "Jubilee." This was celebrated every 50th year. During this time, every man would be able to get his possessions back.

In chapter 26, God discusses the rewards of obedience, and the punishments of disobedience. In verse 1-13, God said that he would send rain. He would grant peace in the land. He would remove evil beasts. He would look on them with respect and make them fruitful. He would keep His covenant with them, and would put His dwelling place among them. He would not hate them, but would walk among them and be their God. If they did not obey, then God would bring on them sudden terror, consumption, and sorrow. If they did not obey, God would set His face against them, and punish them for their sins seven times over. God said that He would break down their stubborn pride. He would bring them bad afflictions seven times over. He would bring the sword upon them, and would send a pestilence upon them. God would be contrary towards them, and would turn their cities against them. Lastly, God would lay desolate their land. God, in His graciousness though, gives Israel instruction to be forgiven. He tells them, as well as us today, that if they will "confess" their sins and the sins of their fathers, that He would remember His covenant with Jacob, Isaac, and Abraham.

Word Study:
 A. Gleanings (23:22)—To pick up after and gather the remains.
 B. Poplars (23:20)—Trees
 C. Sufficient (25:26)—Good enough.
 D. Ruthlessly (25:43)—To be unmerciful
 E. Abhor (26:11)—Hate greatly.
 F. Appalled (26:32)—To be greatly insulted.

Project: Write a 2-3 page paper on one of our holidays (holy-day).
 1. How did it start?
 2. What is it's meaning?
 3. Why do we celebrate it?
 4. Why on that particular day?

Devotional Reading: Leviticus 23:1-27:34

Memory Verse: I Corinthians 16:2

INTRODUCTION TO NUMBERS

Author: Moses
Where Written: Mount Sinai
When: 1445 B. C.
God's Roll: "Counting The Cost!"
God's Command: "Trust Me"
Key Verse: Numbers 10:9; 29
Key Message: God's people must walk by faith, trusting His heart!
Key Word: Faith
Number's Outline:

I.   Waiting (Num. 1-9)
II. Walking (Num. 10-12)
III. Wandering (Num. 13-21)
IV. Waiting (Num. 22-36)

EXTRA NOTES FROM NUMBERS:

Numbers shows that God is the God of trust, and that obedience is the will of God. Numbers is a type of the Christian life. We see here that God offered Israel the land of Canaan, which the chosen people failed to enter because of unbelief. God offers to believers the heavenly land, which may be claimed by the act of faith.

Numbers is about the generation of those who had come out of Egypt. At Mount Sinai, the Jews received the "Law." Here they were organized, consecrated, and instructed. At Kadesh-Barnea, Israel was "inspired" by faith and obedience. In the wilderness journey, Israel was "chastened" by forty years of wandering and death. In Moab, Israel "confesses" their disobedience and is "repaired." **In the Ryrie Study Bible, a five-fold outline is given. It is as follows:**

1. Israel preparing at Sinai
2. Israel marching to Kadesh-Barnea
3. Israel at Kadesh-Barnea
4. Israel marching to Moab
5. Israel on the plains of Moab

Numbers also gives us the "seven murmurings" of Israel in the wilderness. Israel murmured against the way God led them (11:1-3). In 11:4-35, Israel murmured against the food with which God fed them. In 12:1-16, Israel murmured against the authority God set over them. In 13:1-14:38, Israel doubted against the land that God had promised them. In 16:41-50, the Jews fought against the spiritual chastening that God had placed on them. In 20:1-13, Israel complained against the lack of water provided for them. In 21:4-9, Israel complained against the water that God did provide for them.

WAITING AND WALKING

Numbers 1-12

Discussion:

Listed below are the number of fighting men each tribe had before the journey. (Chapter 1)

1.	(20-21)	Reuben	46,500
2.	(22-23)	Simeon	59,300
3.	(24-25)	Gad	45,650
4.	(26-27)	Judah	74,600
5.	(28-29)	Issachar	54,400
6.	(30-31)	Zebulun	57,400
7.	(32-33)	Ephraim	40,500
8.	(34-35)	Manasseh	32,200
9.	(36-37)	Benjamin	35,400
10.	(38-39)	Dan	62,700
11.	(40-41)	Asher	41,500
12.	(42-43)	Naphtali	<u>53,400</u>
	(46)	Grand Total	603,550

The Levites were not counted, for they had no land inheritance, and they were just to minister in the temple.

For an arrangement of the tribes in relation to the temple, please see the section in the book of Exodus on the tabernacle.

Chapter 6 of Numbers, discusses the "Nazarite Vow." This was a vow of separation of a person for the Lord's service. The requirements are seen in verses 3-7. A Nazaritic Vow included a refraining from wine and other fermented drink. It also included not having a razor used on a person's head. A Nazarite was greatly prohibited from going near a dead body or carcass. A Nazarite had to be separated,"wholly unto the Lord." Some examples of men who were Nazaritic were Samson (Judges 13), Samuel (I Samuel 1:9-11), Jesus (Luke 1:15), and Paul (Acts 18:18).

Word Study:
   A. Census (1:2)—To take a count of.
   B. Fermented (6:3)—Wine mixed with alcohol.
   C. Defiling (6:9)—To pollute something.
   D. Ewe (6:14)—A young lamb.

Devotional Reading: Chapter 1,6

Memory Verse: Isaiah 40:31

LESSON 2

WANDERING

Numbers 11-21

Discussion:

In these chapters, we have recorded seven murmurings from the people of Israel against Moses and God. The first murmuring covers from verses one to three. It has to do with the "manna" with which God fed them. God's anger was so kindled that He consumed them with fire. Moses prays, and God stops the fiery terror. In verses 4-35, we have the second murmuring. It was against the "quail" that God fed them. They wanted "flesh" to eat with their bread. Moses then goes to God and complains. Nothing can tear a group or individuals down like negativism, or plain old complaining. When this happens, it must be dealt with quickly and decisively. Moses goes to God and asks Him why He brought this on him. Moses wanted to know what he had done to God to offend Him so much that He would cause the people to complain against Moses. Moses finally said that it was more than he could bear. He tells God that if this is the way He was going to treat him, then to let him die. God then responds and gives Moses 70 elders to help him with the governing of the people. As to the food issue, God decided that He would give the people so much quail, that it would come out of their nostrils! In verse 25, God put a cloud on the 70 men so that they prophesied. Moses then prays and asks God to put His Spirit on everyone. Instead, the Lord strikes the people with a plaque.

In murmuring number three, the people murmur against the "authority" God set over them. This is recorded in 12:1-16. Miriam, Moses' sister and Aaron talk against the decision by Moses to marry a Ethiopian woman. Moses did not argue, for the Bible tells us that Moses was a meek and humble man. God spoke to Moses face to face. God then gives Miriam leprosy, and she is was then put outside of the camp for seven days. The important message here is that God does not like murmuring and will execute his judgment against it.

In murmuring number four, Moses deals with murmuring against the land that God had promised to the children of Israel. This is seen in 13:1-14:38. Moses has 12 men go and check out the promised land and come back and give a report of the land. The conclusion was that it was truly a land flowing with milk and honey, but it was also a land with "great" or giant people. The cities were great and strong-walled. They felt that the land was too hard to possess. They described themselves as "grasshoppers." In chapter 14:4, the report so frightened the people, that they wanted to go back to Egypt. Only two men believed that they could take the land. Joshua and Caleb were optimistic and full of faith in God. God responds, asking Moses, " How long will these people disrespect Me?" He also says, "How long will they refuse to trust in me, in spite of all the miracles I have performed?" Moses prayed and reminded God of the Egyptians and the other nations. In verses 21-23, God would not let them go over into the promised land. Instead, they would wander in the wilderness until they dropped dead. The only men that would enter in would be Joshua and Caleb.

Murmuring number five is against the wilderness journey that God placed on them (16:41-50). The people accused Moses of bringing them out to kill them. In verse 45, God is ready to consume them again. It is amazing the patience that Moses had with these people. Moses then quickly asks Aaron to give an offering of atonement for the sin of the people. That day, 49,700 people die!!

Murmuring number six is against the lack of water provided for them (20:1-13). The people wanted to go back to Egypt. It is also amazing that when we have hard times, how our old life looks better, when in fact it wasn't. God tells Moses to "speak" to a rock. The first time, God told Moses to tap the rock and water gushed out. This time, God tells Moses to speak. Instead, Moses hit's the rock again. This was in direct disobedience to the command of God. Why did Moses do this? He had led an obedient life up to this point. The only reason may be that God wanted us to see that Moses was human, and to see the danger of leadership disobeying God. In verse 12, we probably have some of the saddest words in all the Bible. Moses would not get to go into the promised land! How sad when we see a life of obedience end up in one act of disobedience. But we need to realize that one act of sin can devastate a life. As leaders, we must control our emotions no matter what the situation.

Murmuring number seven is against the water that God did provide for them (21:4-9). The people were getting discouraged and grew tired of the food that God was giving to them. They wanted something else. God sent "fiery serpents" amongst the people to torment and bite them. Moses prayed, and God told him to make a serpent of bronze and put it on a pole. Everyone who looked at this serpent would be healed. This is a type of the crucifixion of Christ. Today, men are sick and need to be healed from the bondage and ravages of sin. "Look to Christ and live" is the church's cry!

Word Study:
   A. Aroused (11:1)—To be stirred up.
   B. Rabble (11:4)—To talk about nothing of importance.
   C. Loathe (11:20)—To hate something sorrowfully.
   D. Prophesied (11:25)—To preach
   E. Leprous (12:10)—To be covered with sores.
   F. Presumption (14:44)—To assume a head of time.
   G. Detest (21:5)—To hate

Devotional Reading: Num. 11-14; 16:41-50; 20:1-13; 21:4-9

Memory Verse: Isaiah 30:21

LESSON 3

WAITING

Numbers 22-36

Discussion:

In chapters 22-24, we see the life of a prophet "for hire." We probably get the word "hireling" from this portion of scripture. Balaam was known as a "mercenary prophet." He was summoned by a Moabite king named Zippor. Zippor wanted Balaam to curse the nation of Israel. God told Balaam not to go with King Zippor. Balaam of course did not listen to God. He set out on his way to Israel. On the way there, an angel with-stood him by standing in the middle of the road.

In verse 23, it was the donkey that saw the angel first.

The donkey would not go down the path and would turn away. Balaam did not see the angel. The first time she turned around, she went off the path into a field. Balaam spanked her back to the path. The second time she went next to a wall. Balaam spanked her again. The next time, she just collapsed under Balaam. He was furious and began to beat the donkey. She finally receives a voice and looks up at Balaam and says, "What have I done unto you that you have whipped me three times?" Balaam's response was that he felt she was being rebellious. She reminded him that there was a angel with a sword standing in the path ready to kill them both. Balaam finally sees the angel, and the angel tells him to say only what God told him to say.

God wanted Balaam to see the blessings of God. God wanted Balaam, like He does all men, to see God's Word as Truth; as a blessing; as a protection and a provision. God wants us to see His word for the nations. What is this Word? It is that God will save all men through Jesus, His Son.

God grants us four things when we hear His Word. He will give us eyes that are opened. He will give us ears to hear His Word. He will give us knowledge to know His Word. He will give us a vision to see Him as He really is. God is the Almighty One!!!

In the second counting of Israel, Moses' count is as follows;

(7)	Reuben	43,730
(14)	Simeon	22,200
(18)	Gad	40,500
(22)	Judah	16,560
(25)	Issachar	4,360
(27)	Zebulun	1,560
(34)	Manasseh	52,700
(37)	Ephraim	32,500
(41)	Benjamin	45,600
(43)	Dan	4,460
(47)	Asher	53,400
(50)	Naphtali	45,400
(51)	Grand Total	601,730

Compared to the first, count there is a 4,000 person difference.

In chapter 27:12-23, we see that Moses is dying, and that God needs to institute a new leader. Moses actually requested a new leader. Moses did not want to leave the people without a shepherd leader. God chose Joshua, because the "Spirit of the Lord" was on him. In verse 23, Moses lays hand on Joshua and commissions Joshua for the service to the Lord. In chapter 35:6-34, God sets up "cities of refuge" for the people. The Levites were given these cities so that if anyone did something wrong or killed someone by mistake, the guilty person could go and get a fair trial.

Word Study:

- A. Horde (22:4)—A group of.
- B. Divination (22:7)—To use magic to determine direction.
- C. Oracle (23:7)— Object of wisdom.
- D. Sorcery (23:23)—Witchcraft
- E. Rouse (23:24)—To stir up.
- F. Prostrate (24:4)—To lay flat on the ground.
- G. Scepter (24:17)—A baton of a king for authority.

Conclusion of the Book: The children of Israel learned that they must trust God and not man in the day of uncertainty and trials; that God would supply all their needs according to His riches ; that they must believe God according to His Word.

Devotional Reading: Num. 22-23; 26; 27:12-23; 35:6-34

Memory Verse: Numbers 23:12

INTRODUCTION TO DEUTERONOMY

Author: Moses
Where Written: Plains of Moab
When: 1405 B.C.
God's Roll: "Restated Again"
God's Command: "Remember"
Key Verse: Deut. 10:12-13
Key Message: the blessedness of obedience and the curse of disobedience.
Key Words: "Trust" and "Obey"
Deuteronomy's Outline:
    I. Israel's History (Chap. 1-4)
    II. Israel's Holiness (Chap. 5-26)
    III. Israel's Hero   (Chap. 27-34)

Notes: Deuteronomy in its very name means "Second Law." It is a book of transition. Deuteronomy is a transition to a new generation. It is a transition to a new law, to a new leader, and to a new way of living. The emphasis of the book is on obedience. Obedience is a necessity because it is the believer's duty before God. The motive of obedience should originate from having a pure heart for God. The standard for obedience comes from a heart that desires to do everything with excellence. The incentive for obedience is to receive the blessings of God. The alternative of obedience is to choose the judgment of God. Deuteronomy was Jesus' favorite book from which to quote.Jesus took it as His code of conduct and ethics (Luke 4:4,8,12). Jesus quoted from it in His conflict with Satan (Mt. 4:4,7,10; Deut. 8:3; 6:16; 110-20).

Another Outline for Deuteronomy is:

I. Moses' First Address - "Looking Back" (Chap. 1-4)

II. Moses' Second Address - "Looking Up" (Chap. 5-26)

III. Moses' Third Address - "Looking Out" (Chap. 27-33)

ISRAEL'S HISTORY AND HOLINESS

Deuteronomy 1-26

Discussion:

Israel's history is reviewed by Moses in an attempt to rouse a spirit of patriotism for their new home and heritage. Chapters 1-4 covers this history lesson. Moses starts off by reminding the Jews to remember the leading of God, in chapters 1-3. In chapter 4:1-8, Moses reminds the Israelites of the Law of God. Moses tells the people that they are to hear the statutes and the judgments of the Lord. The Jews were not to add to, or take away from the "Book of the Law." In observing the law, Israel would show that it surely was a great nation of wisdom and understanding. "What other nation is so great as to have their gods close to them the way the Lord our God is with us whenever we draw close to Him?" What other nation is so great as to have such divine decrees and laws as this body? Moses reminds the people of the commandments of the Lord in verses 9-24 of chapter 4. The people were to obey the laws. If not, they were warned to take heed unto themselves. God is a "consuming fire." Moses then reminds the Jews of the judgment of God (4:25-31). If the people became corrupt, then they would quickly perish, and the Lord would quickly scatter them amongst the nations. Moses told the people not to forget the call of God. Moses told them that it is God that has created man. God spoke to them out of the fire and told the people that He took Israel for Himself, one nation out of another nation. God is the Lord in heaven above and on the earth below.

In chapters 5-26, we have recorded for us the holiness of Israel taught. Chapter five is a restatement of the Law to Israel. The people were to keep these laws in order that everything might go well with them, and that they may dwell in the land and possess it. Israel restates their commitment to One God and His commandments. There were four things that they were do with the Law of God. They were to impress them on their children, talk about them constantly, use them as symbols, and write them on door frames. If Israel kept these laws, it would prove to guide and protect them. Jehovah would be their only true God. God would be their one source of provision. God would be their only source of protection. Israel was called to love this one God only. There is one fundamental fact, and it is this: There is only one God!

There was teaching and preaching concerning marriage. Covenant living affirms that worship is central for a person's life, and that it is consistent with the nature and character of God. Moses taught on the holiness of life (12:1-13:18).He taught on the holiness of food (14:1-21). He taught on the holiness of tithing (14:22-16:22). There was also preaching on leadership. Relationship to authority and authority figures is a troubling issue with which many persons struggle, but never resolve satisfactorily. This teaching focused on the court system, the central temple, and the priest and prophets (17:8-18:22). The rest of Moses' teaching or reviewing centered around four topics; preaching on relationships (19:1-21), preaching on warfare (20:1-20; 21:10-14), preaching on society in conduct (21:1-9, 15-25:19), and preaching on tithing and giving (26:1-19).

Word Study:
- A. Revere (4:10)—To fear with respect.
- B. Awesome (4:34)—Great size, wonderful.
- C. Stipulations (6:17)—Conditions to be met.
- D. Entices (13:6)—To tempt.
- E. Proliferate (21:20)—To raise the level of something.
- F. Purge (21:12)—To cleanse out.

Project: Write 1-2 pages on "Worshipping," What is it? How does one do it? Is it important? Why?

Devotional Reading: Chap. 4;5;6;11;13;21:18-21

Memory Verse: Deuteronomy 34:10

LESSON 2

ISRAEL'S HERO SAYS GOODBYE

Deuteronomy 27-34

Discussion:

God has blessings for us. All we have to do is reach out and take them. If we are not blessed, it is our own fault. God told Israel that all they had to do to have His blessings was to fully hearken to the Lord and follow His commands. God names the blessings in verses 3-6. You will be blessed in the city and in the field. The fruit of your body will be blessed. Your ground and your cattle and sheep will be blessed. You will be blessed when you go out and when you came in. The opposite is expressed in verses 16-19. The reason for the curses would be because they did not serve the Lord their God with joyfulness and gladness in time of blessings. Therefore, in slavery and bondage, in hunger and dire thirst, they would serve the enemies the Lord sends against them.

Chapter 31 is a great chapter in the Old Testament, for it shows the "baton" of leadership being passed on to the next generation leader. This leader's name is Joshua. His name in Hebrew means "Jesus." Moses brings the people together and commands them to be strong and not to be afraid, for God would be with them. God can give promises like this because of who He is. God then tells Joshua to be strong and full of courage. God would be with Joshua as He was with Moses. Joshua is to get all the people together, even the women and the children. They needed to hear the Word of God so that they would fear and know to follow the Lord. God predicts in verse 16 that the people would follow other gods. If they do this, they needed to know that their idol worship would make God angry. This would cause God to hide His face from them. After this, the Levites were instructed to put the Book of the Law in the Ark of the Covenant.

In chapter 34, we watch that great leader Moses die. Moses is buried in the valley of Moab over against Beth-Peor. At the time of his death, Moses was 120 years old. His eye sight was perfect, and his natural strength was still there. Before Moses died, he commissioned Joshua. Verse 9 tells us that the Spirit of the Lord come upon Joshua, and Joshua was filled with the "spirit of wisdom."

According to verse 10, there were two things that were unique about Moses that the Lord leaves for us to see. There was no prophet that had arisen in Israel like Moses whom the Lord knew face to face. Why was Moses a unique man? The answer is given in verse 12. Moses was a mighty man of faith, humility, and steadfastness for God.

Word Study:
   A. Prosperity (28:11)—Abundance
   B. Inflammation (28:22)—Swelling
   C. Festering (28:27)—Building up to draining.
   D. Ravish (28:30)—To take advantage of.
   E. Cultivate (28:39)—To keep working on.
   F. Siege (28:53)—To attack
   G. Begrudge (28:56)- Not wanting the good for someone.
   H. Courageous (31:6)—To be brave.

Project: Look up more verses in the Bible that have to do with "obedience and its promises," and then compare them to verses that have to do with "disobedience and its consequences."

Devotional Reading: Deuteronomy 34:11

Memory Verse: Deuteronomy 34:11

Surveillance
Eric / Erick
#
678 - 457 - 0767